Starting Your Career in

Sport, Entertainment, & Venue Management

Second Edition

Steven Taylor
Matthew Garrett

Kendall Hunt
publishing company

CONTENTS

SECTION 4 – AFTER THE HIRE   109

SECTION 5 – BUILDING ON THE EXPERIENCE   141

FOREWORD

If you want to work in the sport, entertainment, and venue industry, you need to read this book and apply its lessons. Like some other books it will help you identify numerous career paths—some that you never knew about—and describe some of the duties of each job. Unlike other books, it will actually lead you step-by-step in preparing to compete for the scarce and desirable jobs in this business segment. It will tell you not just what to do but how to do it in a way that professionals value.

When I left the business after nearly 30 years to join the faculty of the Department of Sport and Entertainment Management at the University of South Carolina, I didn't really know WHY I was doing that or what my role might be. It didn't take long for me to discover my mission: helping mold better entry-level employees for an industry that had been really good to me. Every organization in sport, entertainment, and venue management struggles to find employees who "get it." Many people seek these positions in a quest to be part of the thrilling excitement they experience as fans. Very few have any idea what working in this industry is really like. Even fewer are willing to put in the effort required. The demands lead to high turnover; turnover is very expensive. I wanted to find ways to reduce turnover for businesses by graduating students who understood what it meant to work in this industry and had developed the necessary aptitude and attitude to succeed in it.

To accomplish this, it was imperative to have an Internship Director who shared my vision and who could "walk the walk." Steve Taylor was both an undergraduate and graduate student of mine who essentially created a job for himself out of his internship in the athletics department of a small college. When I got the opportunity to hire a new Internship Director, Steve Taylor was my first choice. He understood what it meant to work in this industry;

he had the aptitude and the attitude to succeed in it; he wanted to help others succeed in it. When he was hired, I tasked Steve with revamping an already successful internship program to make it even more rigorous to help really pound home the lessons that needed to be learned. To say he succeeded is a huge understatement. In addition to the gratitude of his former students, he has earned accolades and respect from business leaders, some of whom you will meet in the following chapters.

In this book, Steve Taylor shares with the reader his well-constructed plan that prepares one to get a job in this industry and succeed at the entry level—the most frequent point of failure. Following the plan will not be quick, and it will not be easy. One cannot just read the lessons and tasks thinking "Oh yeah, I can do that when the time comes." To succeed you must follow the step-by-step plan he has developed. If you do everything he tells you to do, strive for excellence while doing it, and seek to understand why it is important, you will be well on your way to competing successfully for one of the scarce jobs in the exciting world of sport, entertainment, and venue management. Anyone considering working in this industry should read this book.

Frank Roach spent 12 years teaching future professionals, three as interim Chair, in the Sport and Entertainment Management program at the University of South Carolina. Frank's industry experience spans five decades, starting at the Hampton Coliseum in 1975. He was Feld Entertainment's Vice President for Routing and Tours for 15 years and spent time at MCA/Universal Concerts, TourVen Inc., and SFX/Clear Channel. Frank also taught a generation of venue professionals at IAVM's Venue Management School.

As I reflect upon my career journey thus far, it is clear that experiential learning played an integral role in the start of that journey. At Loras College, I quickly zeroed in on sport management as my major but was unsure what a career in sports could look like for me. Luckily both the program and Dr. Matt Garrett prioritized experiential learning. In addition to many real-world class projects, I also had the opportunity to complete several internships. These internships provided not only practical work experience but also exposure to areas of sport. I was able to learn about college athletics and event management – to see what I liked and, perhaps more importantly, did not like. I began to understand the skills that I would need to succeed.

However, it was my final internship that was the most pivotal in my journey. Prior to my senior year, I completed a three-month internship in junior golf. I helped run junior golf events. This included everything from paperwork, to on-course rulings, to customer support and much more. This experience opened my eyes to the world of golf administration. Prior to the internship, my knowledge of the golf industry stopped at what I saw on TV and experienced in my own playing. Through this experience I learned the industry was far more extensive and found my passion. After graduation, I was fortunate to start my career at the United States Golf Association (USGA) where I've continued to work for the last five years.

I often think of how valuable experiential learning was to me. I am grateful that Dr. Garrett stressed its importance to me and to all of his students. He continues to incorporate experiential learning in a valuable way for his students. I hope that all students who read this book can gain the same appreciation and understand the importance of these opportunities. It is these opportunities that will lay the foundation for the next steps of their career journeys.

Kathryn Belanger is an Assistant Director for Rules Education and Engagement with the United States Golf Association

Contributed by Kathryn Belanger. © Kendall Hunt Publishing Company.

ABOUT THE AUTHORS

Steve Taylor is a Senior Instructor and, since 2008, the Director of Internships for the Sport and Entertainment Management Department at the University of South Carolina. He has led student experiential learning classes to the European Athletics Championships, the Commonwealth Games, two Olympic Games, the Kentucky Derby, and the Firefly Music Festival to name a few.

Steve and his wife Kristen have three children and six grandchildren and live in Lexington, SC.

Matt Garrett is a professor of sport management at Loras College. His students won ten academic case study championships at national conferences in the past decade. He supervises the internship program and his students have pursued opportunities in multiple industry segments and across the globe. He has also authored journal articles on the job trajectory for sport management graduates.

Garrett is a member of the City of Dubuque's Park and Leisure Commission and he has previous experience as president of Dubuque Little League and as a women's basketball coach at Blackburn College. He and his wife Cheryl have three kids and live in Dubuque.

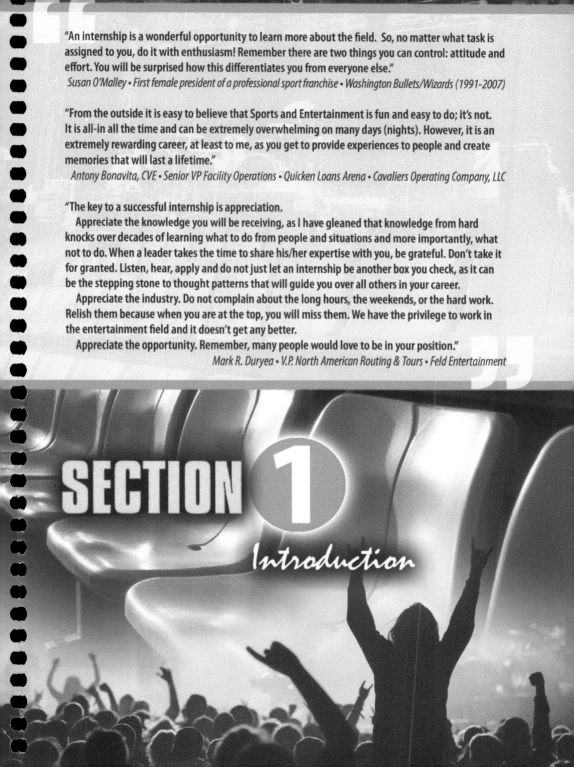

"An internship is a wonderful opportunity to learn more about the field. So, no matter what task is assigned to you, do it with enthusiasm! Remember there are two things you can control: attitude and effort. You will be surprised how this differentiates you from everyone else."

Susan O'Malley • First female president of a professional sport franchise • Washington Bullets/Wizards (1991-2007)

"From the outside it is easy to believe that Sports and Entertainment is fun and easy to do; it's not. It is all-in all the time and can be extremely overwhelming on many days (nights). However, it is an extremely rewarding career, at least to me, as you get to provide experiences to people and create memories that will last a lifetime."

Antony Bonavita, CVE • Senior VP Facility Operations • Quicken Loans Arena • Cavaliers Operating Company, LLC

"The key to a successful internship is appreciation.

Appreciate the knowledge you will be receiving, as I have gleaned that knowledge from hard knocks over decades of learning what to do from people and situations and more importantly, what not to do. When a leader takes the time to share his/her expertise with you, be grateful. Don't take it for granted. Listen, hear, apply and do not just let an internship be another box you check, as it can be the stepping stone to thought patterns that will guide you over all others in your career.

Appreciate the industry. Do not complain about the long hours, the weekends, or the hard work. Relish them because when you are at the top, you will miss them. We have the privilege to work in the entertainment field and it doesn't get any better.

Appreciate the opportunity. Remember, many people would love to be in your position."

Mark R. Duryea • V.P. North American Routing & Tours • Feld Entertainment

SECTION 1

Introduction

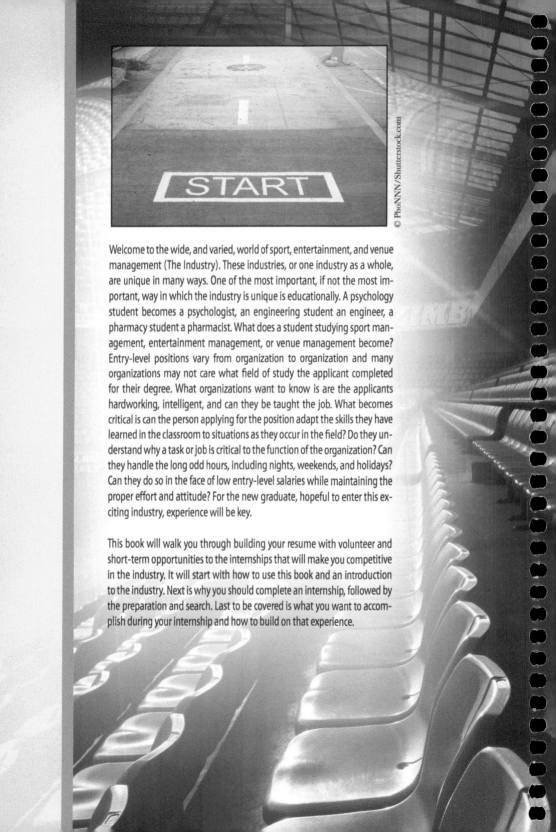

Welcome to the wide, and varied, world of sport, entertainment, and venue management (The Industry). These industries, or one industry as a whole, are unique in many ways. One of the most important, if not the most important, way in which the industry is unique is educationally. A psychology student becomes a psychologist, an engineering student an engineer, a pharmacy student a pharmacist. What does a student studying sport management, entertainment management, or venue management become? Entry-level positions vary from organization to organization and many organizations may not care what field of study the applicant completed for their degree. What organizations want to know is are the applicants hardworking, intelligent, and can they be taught the job. What becomes critical is can the person applying for the position adapt the skills they have learned in the classroom to situations as they occur in the field? Do they understand why a task or job is critical to the function of the organization? Can they handle the long odd hours, including nights, weekends, and holidays? Can they do so in the face of low entry-level salaries while maintaining the proper effort and attitude? For the new graduate, hopeful to enter this exciting industry, experience will be key.

This book will walk you through building your resume with volunteer and short-term opportunities to the internships that will make you competitive in the industry. It will start with how to use this book and an introduction to the industry. Next is why you should complete an internship, followed by the preparation and search. Last to be covered is what you want to accomplish during your internship and how to build on that experience.

CHAPTER 1

Using this Book

Once again welcome to the wide world that is sport, entertainment, and venue management. Sport, entertainment, and venue management are considered one and the same for the purposes of this book. The term "industry" will be used to refer to all three and the entertainment component is meant to be all forms of live entertainment. The reason for this is simple, for what is sport but a form of entertainment—whether playing or watching. Neither a sporting event nor an entertainment event could be held without a venue of some sort. Many of the skills needed to succeed in one area are transferable to another. If you can sell tickets to a football game, you can sell them to a concert. If you can market a family show, you can do the same for a music festival.

© Rawpixel.com/Shutterstock.com

In this industry you learn by doing and nowhere is there more potential to learn than in an internship. This book is designed to help the student through what may seem a daunting task, preparing for, finding, securing, and learning from a meaningful internship experience. The book may be used in conjunction with a class, or classes, in a relevant academic curriculum with an internship component, whether the internship is required or encouraged. The book is also meant for the student whose program does not have an internship component or a student who is not enrolled in a relevant academic program. Truly anyone who wants to start a career in sport, entertainment, or venue management can use this book to start their journey.

You will read, through these pages, some themes that may seem redundant. These often-repeated concepts are critical for the student to understand and internalize to be truly successful in this industry. There is no magic carpet to carry you where you want to be. It will take hard work, a great attitude, and a passion to be where you are. There will be times when even that will not be enough and the only recourse is to start again. Following along in this book and completing the tasks given will guide you on this trip and help focus your energies in the correct direction.

For the student in an academic program offering an internship program simply follow along in the book as is prescribed by your instructor or professor. For the student who does not have the benefit of an internship program or is earning a degree in a non-industry specific program (i.e. Marketing, Management, Business Administration) the best way to use this book is to read it completely first. This will give you an overall view of what you are trying to accomplish. Once that is complete, you should begin following the steps outlined in the book, completing the tasks in order with the culmination being the completion of a successful internship. This will not be a quick process and may require the repeat of one or many steps or one or more academic sessions, semesters, or quarters depending on your institution's academic calendar. It is not a simple process, but it is one you should be excited to undertake and enjoy completing.

Starting Your Career in Sport, Entertainment, & Venue Management

CHAPTER 2

Introduction to the Sport, Entertainment, and Venue Industry

The sport, entertainment, and venue management industry is a wide, varied, and unique field to work in. According to the United States Department of Labor, the industry is growing faster than all other occupations, increasing at a rate of about ten percent (79,600 new jobs) from 2016 to 2026. What it is not is large, with a total of less than one million jobs. By comparison the hospitality industry employs more than 14 million people. The sport, entertainment, and venue industry is also very popular on college campuses, with programs at over 400 institutions nationwide. If each program produces just 25 graduates per year, and quite a few produce many more, that is 10,000 new

© Hollygraphic/Shutterstock.com

potential employees entering the job market every year. This is a highly competitive field with the potential for hundreds of applicants for the most popular jobs.

One of many things that makes the industry unique, and which makes the experiential learning of an internship so important, is the diversity of tasks that can be assigned and the similar answer to almost every problem you will face as an industry professional. Regardless of position, almost every question has the same answer, it depends. You will need to apply what you have learned in the classroom but how you apply it will come from experience. The experience you gain doing the job and learning from those who have done the job will be needed to apply to the problem, or question, at hand. For many problems there will be no "book" answer and you will have to do what "feels" right based on those experiences.

> Example 1: You are the box office manager and you are working on scaling the house for a concert. How should you price the tickets to the concert? It depends. Who is the act? What is the seating arrangement? How many tickets can we sell? What is our demographic? What is the economic climate? What other events are we competing with? These are just a few of the questions that need answering before you can answer the first one.

> Example 2: You are working for a minor league franchise. Tonight's bobblehead promotion has created a buzz and a long line awaits the opening of the gates. You are talking with fans and soon recognize that your advertising efforts stated that the first 2,000 people through the gates will receive the souvenir, though you know there are only 1,000 bobbleheads to distribute. How do you solve this problem? It depends. You will not make everyone who does not receive a bobblehead happy, so what is the goal of the damage control? Appease those you can? Retain as many fans as possible? Somewhere in a closet is your promotions swag. Do you have enough of another item to meet demand and the stated number of giveaways? Do you have the capacity, both manpower and financial, to capture all the fans who should have received bobbleheads and mail them bobbleheads from a reorder? Do you even overly concern yourself with the upset fans? Are they one-time fans who would most likely not return anyway? These are some of the questions that need answering in the spur of the moment as you try to decide the best course of action.

© Photobank gallery/Shutterstock.com

Example 3: You are the marketing assistant for a lower-tier bowl game played the day after Christmas. What is your plan? With such a broad question it depends on many things. Do I know who is in the game? Has my local community supported the game in the past? Am I in a destination city where I can sell the game as a Christmas vacation? How many butts-in-seats do I need? All the economic questions, local and national, in the locale of the teams playing. What is my budget? And this is only a quick start to all the factors that will impact your plan.

As you can see the "it depends" answer will be repeated over and over during your career. Classes cannot truly teach you how to deal with pricing issues or angry fans but they will give you a basis, a toolbox if you will, to use to solve the problems. Your marketing class will certainly give you the theory, the "tools," to ask the right questions to get you the information that you need. In all situations it will be up to you to apply what you have learned, based on your and others' experiences, to the unique problem at hand. You can only do this by doing, and by learning from those who have done before.

Ultimately everyone using this book has the same outcome in mind for the culmination of their academic career, an entry-level job in the industry. As such a few words here should be used to describe what that may be like. Your first job in the industry will be very similar to your internship experience in that you will work a lot of hours. Those hours may very well be worked at times when others are enjoying themselves: nights, weekends, and holidays. Your initial pay will not be large either and may very well be less than your peers in other businesses. Much of this is because demand for these jobs is so high and turnover so great. This industry is not for everyone and, while the "passion" and drive many feel at the beginning is great, it is worn away quickly by the grind the job may become. Because of this, organizations do not pay a great deal as they know there is a new crop of applicants waiting for their chance.

Perhaps the best way to describe the process is through an analogy. Working in this industry is a great deal like being an undrafted rookie free agent in an NFL training camp. Yes, that rookie will make more money than you, the entry-level employee, but he makes much less than drafted rookies and returning veterans. What is the job of an undrafted rookie free agent in camp? Why does the organization bring them on? They are an inexpensive way to help prepare the players who will make the team (or are expected to make the team). They give the organization the bodies needed to properly prepare without overloading the regulars. As a secondary benefit they allow the organization to identify new talent who may be able to assist the organization in achieving its goals. These undrafted rookies are cannon fodder for the regulars to beat up on to get themselves ready. As for the undrafted rookies—they just want a chance to show that they can help, and, on occasion, some are kept on and develop into contributors.

Again, the pay scale is much different but the principle is the same. As an entry-level employee you are there to provide the organization with a benefit, your labor, in the hope that the organization can identify talent that can be productive long term. They, the organization, wants employees who can handle the grind and excel. They are looking for you to have a great attitude, put forth great effort, and thrive in what can sometimes be chaos. This is why, especially in sports, many organizations hire so many seasonal and part-time workers, a typical entry-level position. They need to know the new employee can handle the rigors before they truly invest in the training and salary for a new hire. If you do keep that positive attitude and give the great effort needed you can find yourself moving up rapidly to better jobs and better pay.

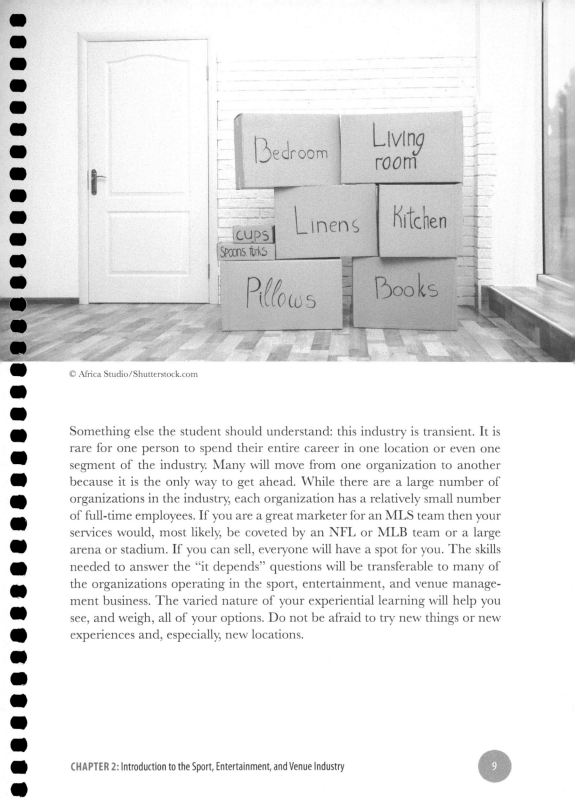

© Africa Studio/Shutterstock.com

Something else the student should understand: this industry is transient. It is rare for one person to spend their entire career in one location or even one segment of the industry. Many will move from one organization to another because it is the only way to get ahead. While there are a large number of organizations in the industry, each organization has a relatively small number of full-time employees. If you are a great marketer for an MLS team then your services would, most likely, be coveted by an NFL or MLB team or a large arena or stadium. If you can sell, everyone will have a spot for you. The skills needed to answer the "it depends" questions will be transferable to many of the organizations operating in the sport, entertainment, and venue management business. The varied nature of your experiential learning will help you see, and weigh, all of your options. Do not be afraid to try new things or new experiences and, especially, new locations.

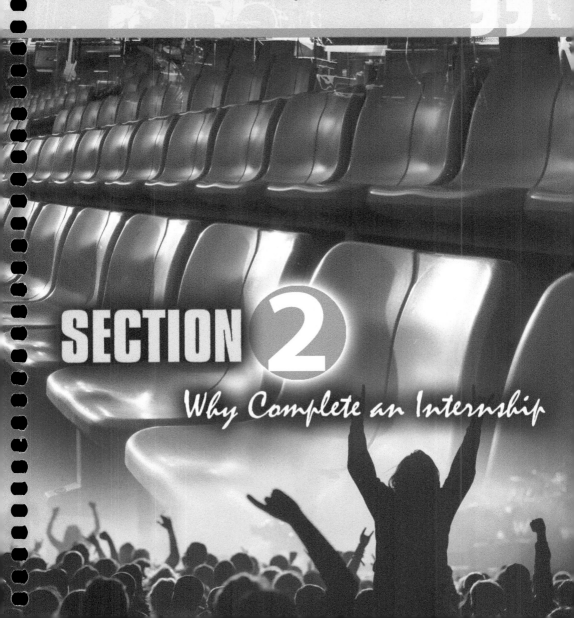

"Your career is what you are paid for; your calling is what you are made for. Try different avenues until you find your calling. Be honest with yourself if this industry is not the right fit for you."

Jana N. Brooks • Coordinator, Events & Tenant Services • Maryland Stadium Authority

"I look for characteristics that show the candidate has taken initiative to get involved and gain experience outside of the classroom. That could be in the form of internships, volunteer work or other paid job experience."

Josh Harris •Senior Director, Ticketing & Guest Services • Daytona International Speedway

SECTION 2

Why Complete an Internship

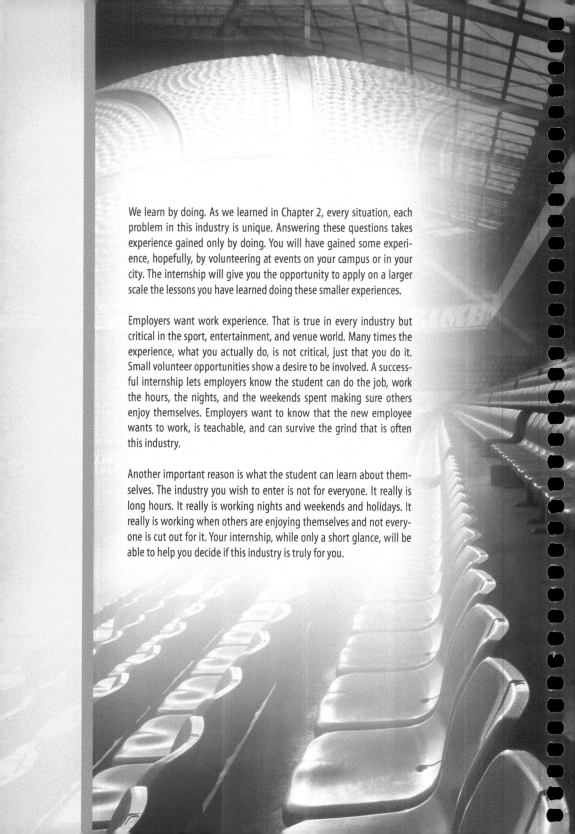

We learn by doing. As we learned in Chapter 2, every situation, each problem in this industry is unique. Answering these questions takes experience gained only by doing. You will have gained some experience, hopefully, by volunteering at events on your campus or in your city. The internship will give you the opportunity to apply on a larger scale the lessons you have learned doing these smaller experiences.

Employers want work experience. That is true in every industry but critical in the sport, entertainment, and venue world. Many times the experience, what you actually do, is not critical, just that you do it. Small volunteer opportunities show a desire to be involved. A successful internship lets employers know the student can do the job, work the hours, the nights, and the weekends spent making sure others enjoy themselves. Employers want to know that the new employee wants to work, is teachable, and can survive the grind that is often this industry.

Another important reason is what the student can learn about themselves. The industry you wish to enter is not for everyone. It really is long hours. It really is working nights and weekends and holidays. It really is working when others are enjoying themselves and not everyone is cut out for it. Your internship, while only a short glance, will be able to help you decide if this industry is truly for you.

CHAPTER 3

The Internship as an Integral Part of the Curriculum

As a student enrolled in a sport, entertainment, venue management or related academic program, you have a great opportunity to gain insight from your faculty members and classmates as you prepare for your internship and subsequent career path.

© phloxii/Shutterstock.com

The internship experience is a necessary and integral component of a sport management degree curriculum. Your curriculum often begins with an introductory course, or courses, that may include only other aspiring sport management majors or that may be a broader offering that purposefully includes kinesiology, business, or physical education majors as a general introduction to a division or school of sport studies, kinesiology, or business. This class should allow you to determine if the sport and entertainment business is an area you want to continue to study and build a career around. You should have the chance to learn what you can expect from your institution's internship program. Take advantage of meeting other students at your school who have completed the internship experience, either formally through student club functions or classes or informally as opportunities arise. These upper-class students are a great resource and can offer guidance on how internships are preparing them for future success in their professional endeavors and goals.

Your curriculum, after the introduction course, will keep you on a proper path to building your content knowledge. You should look to complete multiple experiences (short and long-term volunteer positions and internships) with varying degrees of responsibility and at different times throughout your curricular experience. Ideally these experiences will also represent different industry segments. These may be for elective credit, credit within your degree program satisfying a graduation requirement, or no credit at all. It will be incumbent on you to research the curriculum or talk with an academic advisor to learn more about the particulars of credit opportunities at your institution.

© GUGAI/Shutterstock.com

You should consider an internship experience when you are still early in your academic career. This should be an experience where you get introduced to different facets of an organization in a professional setting. Your interpersonal skills and professional dispositions will still be developing and in need of practice. You may not yet have advanced knowledge in areas such as marketing or finance, but you should have a basic knowledge of them. In the proper setting and with the proper mentoring you will have the opportunity to grow in all areas.

Depending on your institution and the proximity to different sport and entertainment businesses and venues, and your own course schedule, you can complete multiple experiences through the beginning of your junior year. These can include summers and mini-mesters as your institution offers. You must be proactive in contacting the appropriate individuals who can assist you. You also should work with campus professionals on building your resume. It is likely you will be competing with upper-class students even for these smaller opportunities, so you must find a way to distinguish yourself. As you will read in Chapter 5, make sure to volunteer at events as much as possible.

Once you have reached your junior year, approximately, you will be taking industry-specific classes such as law, finance, economics, social issues, governance, marketing, sales, and others as your curriculum provides. You will also be taking supporting coursework in business or other related fields. You may or may not take these courses in any particular order. Management in these industries is not as dependent on the building-block theory as other disciplines, meaning a certain content area does not necessarily have to be mastered for a student to advance in a program.

Once you have taken enough coursework and participated in volunteer, classroom, or small internship opportunities, you should be ready to participate in a larger internship experience that serves as a capstone experience. The Commission of Sport Management Accreditation's document "Accreditation Principles and Self Study Preparation May 2016" identifies the internship/practical/experiential learning experience as a necessary integrative experience which institutions must demonstrate that they offer when seeking accreditation.

You should be able to identify how things learned in the classroom play out in the practical setting. Maybe in a marketing class you completed a promotions grid where you had to determine which games or events matched with the best promotions. Can you apply this to your internship organization? Maybe in a law class you had to visit a park or other recreational facility and identify all potential hazards as part of a risk management plan. Can you assist your internship venue in making a review of such hazards? Maybe a guest speaker in one of your classes was a young professional telling you about some of the sacrifices made in their personal life working 12-game baseball home stands. Can you make those same sacrifices?

Either way you will be facing similar experiences in your internships. You should have conversations with co-workers, fellow interns, and mentors about how your classroom learning correlates with your work experiences. Conversely, you should be talking to your professors about the same things.

CHAPTER 4

Defined Industries

This book includes sport, entertainment, and venue management as if they are one field. If you are in a sport, entertainment, or venue management program you will be educated on what each means to your program and professors. However, this book may be used by those not in such a program and this chapter will give a brief overview of the wide-ranging opportunities in this industry. There is significant debate as to what construes a sport. Some scholars believe the competitive atmosphere and a definite winner are the predominant factors in the definition. Others stipulate there must be an athletic component. Most will agree, though, that sport is just another form of live entertainment, and no live show, be it sport, a concert, or a family show, can happen without a venue.

The arguments over the definition of sport are not necessarily important for the purpose of your internship search or your future job search. What is important is that each of the types of entities listed below can offer a functional area (covered in Chapter 7) with a business component where students can find successful internships and subsequent careers.

SPORT

Ask a student what they want to do in sport and you hear answers like I want to be a general manager, an agent, a scout. Ask them in what sport they want to lead, represent athletes, or scout and they may tell you something like either the NFL or the NBA or they may even say it does not really matter. Professional sport is not the only "game" in town. Recreational, scholastic, and amateur sports are a huge industry as well. It is important that you expand your view of what organizations are potential landing spots for your talents. This includes expanding to a global view as well. Sport entities that may want and need your talents include:

- Professional Sport Franchises and Leagues – The top 20 revenue leagues in the world include all the major U.S. leagues as well as the rest of the world's "football" leagues, including the Australian Football League, and generate $40 billion in revenue each year. Besides the North American members of the top 20, National Football League (NFL), Major League Baseball (MLB), National Basketball Association (NBA), National Hockey League (NHL), and Major League Soccer (MLS), there are other top-level professional leagues, including:
  - o Women's National Basketball Association
  - o Arena Football League
  - o National Women's Soccer League
  - o National Lacrosse League
  - o Major League Lacrosse
  - o Major League Rugby
  - o Canadian Women's Hockey League
  - o National Women's Hockey League
  - o Canadian Football League

© Istvan Hajas/Shutterstock.com

Starting Your Career in Sport, Entertainment, & Venue Management

North America is also home to a large number of minor leagues and minor league teams. These organizations can offer substantial opportunity because they tend to be all-hands-on-deck in their operations with everyone doing a little bit of everything. The way to the "Bigs" may be through the minors for you—just like for players. These minor leagues (as of the printing of this book) include:

o Baseball – 250 plus minor league organizations
o Soccer – USL Championship League (USLC), North American Soccer League (NASL), USL League One, USL League Two, National Premier Soccer League, United Women's Soccer (UWS), Women's Premier Soccer League (WPSL)
o Hockey – American Hockey League (AHL), ECHL (formerly East Coast Hockey League), Southern Professional Hockey League (SPHL), Federal Hockey League (FHL), and Ligue Nord-Américaine de Hockey (LNAH)
o Basketball – NBA G League, American Basketball Association (ABA), American Professional Basketball League (APBL), Central Basketball Association (CBA), East Coast Basketball League (ECBL), Elite Basketball League (EBL), Florida Basketball Association (FBA), Midwest Basketball League (MBL), North American Basketball League (NABL), The Basketball League (TBL), United Basketball League (UBL), Universal Basketball Association (UBA)
o Football – Arena Football League (AFL), Champions Indoor Football (CIF), Indoor Football League (IFL), National Arena League (NAL), XFL (beginning play in 2020 in eight cities)

© onot/Shutterstock.com

If you are interested in working abroad, there are numerous sports and organizations both similar and different from North American sports. The sports you are familiar with are:

o Baseball – played around the world in leagues such as:
   - Dominican Summer League
   - Mexican League
   - Panamanian Professional Baseball League
   - Asia Winter Baseball League – Multinational
   - Australian Baseball League
   - KBO League – South Korea
   - Nippon Professional Baseball – Japan
   - Italian Baseball League
   - Honkbal Hoofdklasse – Netherlands
o Basketball – played around the world in leagues such as:
   - Africa – FIBA Africa Clubs Champions Cup (Multinational), Egyptian Basketball Super League, Basketball National League (South Africa), Angolan Basketball League
   - Americas – FIBA Americas League (Multinational), Liga Nacional de Básquet (Argentina), Campeonato Brasileiro de Basquete (Brazil), National Basketball League of Canada (NBLC), Liga Profesional de Baloncesto (Panama)
   - Asia – FIBA Asia Champions Cup (Multinational), Chinese Basketball Association (CBA), B.League (Japan), UAE National Basketball League (United Arab Emirates)
   - Europe – FIBA EuroBasket (Multinational), EuroLeague (Multinational Clubs), A-1 Liga (Croatia), Ligue Nationale de Basketball Pro A (France), Basketball Bundesliga (Germany), Lietuvos Krepšinio Lyga (LKL Lithuania), Dutch Basketball League (Netherlands)
   - Oceania – National Basketball League (NBL Australia and New Zealand)
   - Women's Leagues – There are numerous women's leagues around the world as well, like the Women's Hong Kong Basketball Association, Women's Japan Basketball League, Zenith Women Basketball League (ZWBL Nigeria), Austrian Women's Basketball Bundesliga, Ligue Féminine de Basketball (France), Lega Basket Femminile Serie A1 (Italy), and the Women's National Basketball League (Australia and New Zealand)

© PopTika/Shutterstock.com

o   Other sports with professional leagues worldwide include (this is
      not a comprehensive list):
   –   American Football – Canada, India, Germany, and Mexico
   –   Cricket – with leagues in Africa, Asia, North America,
        Europe, and Oceania
   –   Field Hockey – India, Malaysia, Pakistan, Euro Hockey
        League (Multinational), Netherlands, Australia
   –   Ice Hockey – Played in North America, most of Europe,
        and in Asia and Oceania
   –   Kabaddi – World
        League (Multinational)
   –   Netball – Australia and
        New Zealand
   –   Rugby League – Aus-
        tralia, France, England,
        India, New Zealand,
        Papua New Guinea,
        Russia, U.S.

© Studio_G/Shutterstock.com

- Rugby Union – Australia, Fiji, U.S., Canada, England, France, Ireland, South Africa, Namibia, New Zealand, Russia, Wales
- Softball – U.S., U.K., India
- Volleyball/Beach Volleyball – U.S., China, Greece, Dominican Republic, Russia, Brazil, Italy
- Water Polo – Australia, Italy, Greece

Professional sports teams and leagues are worldwide and incredibly diverse in their offerings. That, however, is not the end of the professional offerings in this industry. You have:

o Golf – played professional on multiple levels around the world. The top-level tours:
- PGA Tour (United States)
- PGA European Tour
- Japan Golf Tour
- Asian Tour (Asia outside Japan)
- PGA Tour of Australasia (Australia and New Zealand)
- Sunshine Tour (southern Africa, mainly South Africa)
- OneAsia Tour (joint venture among the Japan, Australasia, China, and Korean tours)
- Professional Golf Tour of India
- PGA Tour Champions (United States)
- European Senior Tour

Developmental tours:
- Web.com Tour (second-tier U.S. tour, operated by the PGA Tour)
- Challenge Tour (second-tier European tour)
- Japan Challenge Tour (second-tier Japanese tour)
- PGA Tour Canada (feeds to the Web.com Tour)
- PGA Tour China (feeds to the Web.com Tour)
- PGA Tour Latinoamérica (feeds to the Web.com Tour)
- Gateway Tour (third-tier U.S. tour)
- Fuzion Minor League Golf Tour (low-cost fourth-tier U.S. tour)
- SwingThought Tour (third-tier U.S. tour)

Women's tours:
- LPGA (Ladies Professional Golf Association; United States)
- LPGA of Japan Tour
- Ladies European Tour

© kayannl/Shutterstock.com

- LPGA of Korea Tour (South Korea)
- Ladies Asian Golf Tour (Asia outside Japan and Korea)
- ALPG Tour (Australia)
- Legends Tour (United States)

Women's developmental tours:
- Symetra Tour (second-tier U.S. tour, operated by the LPGA)
- Ladies European Tour Access Series, LETAS (feeder tour to the Ladies European Tour)
- Step Up Tour (second-tier Japanese tour, operated by the LPGA of Japan)
- Swedish Golf Tour (women's version is a second-tier tour in Sweden, feeding to the Ladies European Tour)

o Tennis
- Association of Tennis Professionals
- International Tennis Federation
- United States Tennis Association
- Women's Tennis Association
- World Team Tennis

o Combat Sports
- Boxing – There are numerous sanctioning bodies (WBA, WBO, WBC, IBF) and a large number of major promotion companies such as Top Rank Boxing, Golden Boy Promotions, and DiBella Entertainment
- Kickboxing – organizations like Glory, K-1, Kunlun Fight
- Mixed Martial Arts – like other combat sports there are a

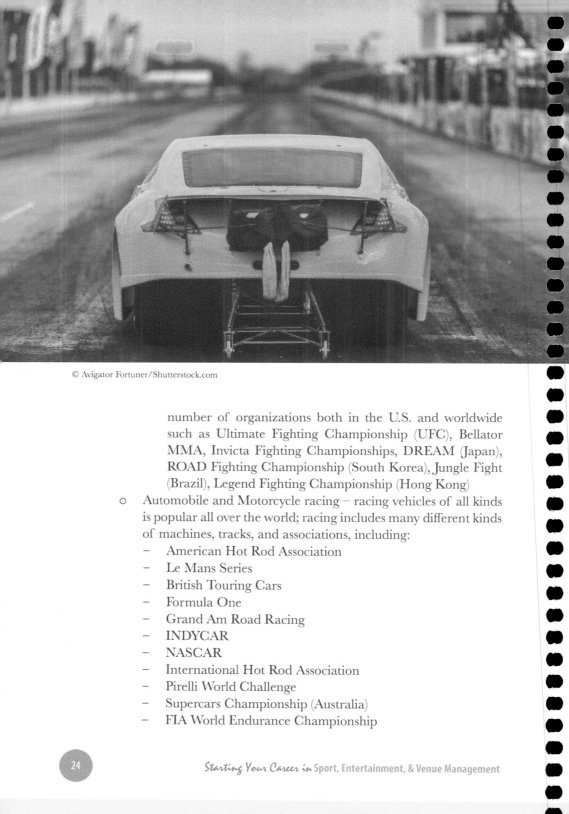

© Avigator Fortuner/Shutterstock.com

number of organizations both in the U.S. and worldwide such as Ultimate Fighting Championship (UFC), Bellator MMA, Invicta Fighting Championships, DREAM (Japan), ROAD Fighting Championship (South Korea), Jungle Fight (Brazil), Legend Fighting Championship (Hong Kong)

o Automobile and Motorcycle racing – racing vehicles of all kinds is popular all over the world; racing includes many different kinds of machines, tracks, and associations, including:
- American Hot Rod Association
- Le Mans Series
- British Touring Cars
- Formula One
- Grand Am Road Racing
- INDYCAR
- NASCAR
- International Hot Rod Association
- Pirelli World Challenge
- Supercars Championship (Australia)
- FIA World Endurance Championship

Starting Your Career in Sport, Entertainment, & Venue Management

- World Rally Championship
- There are also professional events, and tours, for what some may consider recreational sports.
- Bowling – Professional Bowlers Association
- Darts – Professional Darts Corporation
- Billiards – World Pool-Billiard Association

Extreme sports, such as those presented by ESPN's X Games and also included in the Olympics, continue to grow. The action will vary from event to event and include events such as the following:

- Skateboarding events, including Big Air, Street, and Skateboard Park
- BMX bike events, including BMX Park, BMX Vert, and Street
- Moto X events, including Quarter Pipe, Big Air, and Freestyle
- Rally Car Racing
- Surfing
- Snowboard and Ski events, including Slopestyle, Knuckle Huck, and SuperPipe
- Snowmobile events, including Best Trick and Freestyle

Every year new sports emerge and work their way on to broadcasts such as ESPN 8: The Ocho. Recent years have seen the return of playground games such as Dodgeball and the introduction of competitive professional leagues. Each of these sports and events will have the same types of operational positions as other "mainstream" sport. This is an ever-evolving category and, as of this printing, includes properties such as the following:

- Karate combat
- Spikeball
- Pickleball
- Cornhole
- Beach soccer
- Axe throwing
- Break dancing
- Marble league

While this list is in no way inclusive of every professional sport entity there is, it is meant to show you that there is much more to the world of professional sport than just a few "major league" franchises. Each of these entities can offer opportunity for a student who is willing to go "outside the box" to find their future.

ESPORTS

Esports is a rapidly growing segment for those who want to work in the industry. Esports opportunities include positions with publishers, professional teams, leagues, and venues. There are also amateur leagues, collegiate leagues, and even high school leagues. Esports, as of this publication, continue to grow rapidly and offer opportunity to those entering the work world particularly as the industry continues to mature and become more formalized. Because so many positions are new, they tend to skew younger as well.

This industry segment is, and will continue to be, evolving as it grows and matures. Opportunity also exists, because of this dynamic nature, to move from one facet of esports to another. The lists below are only a small portion of the industry and do not include all entities of any category.

Publishers are the organizations that create the games. Beyond that the publishers also host competitions, produce relevant coverage, and license their products to external entities who produce competitions.

- Activision
- Riot
- Epic
- Valve
- Nintendo
- EA
- Ubisoft

Major Games

- League of Legends
- CS:GO
- Overwatch
- Call of Duty
- Rocket League
- Valorant
- DoTA 2
- StarCraft II
- Fortnite
- Super Smash Brothers
- Madden
- Rainbow Six Siege

Tournament and League organizers run their own competitions as well as the coverage of the contests. They may sell the broadcasts to streaming services as well. These events may be both watched in person and live streamed.

- Overwatch League
- NBA 2K League
- Call of Duty League
- eMLS League
- NA LCS League

Franchise Teams may have numerous squads who play different games. They may also have developmental squads or all-female squads. Teams may be sponsored by publishers or other outside organizations.

- Dallas Fuel—Overwatch
- FlyQuest—League of Legends
- Houston Outlaws—Overwatch
- FC Schalke 04—Soccer
- MiBR—Counter-Strike
- Polar Ace—Counter-Strike

Purpose-built esports venues are being opened around the world. Hosting esports competitions is also a source of revenue for many multiuse facilities. Just a few years ago, esports was not a central function of these multiuse venues but is now a valued revenue stream for facilities struggling to make ends meet.

- Fusion Arena—Philadelphia, Pennsylvania
- The Esports Arena—Santa Ana, California
- Chongqing Zhongxian E-Sports Stadium—Zhongxian, ChongQing, China
- Gfinity Arena—London, England
- LVL—Berlin, Germany
- HyperX Esports Arena—Las Vegas, Nevada
- Esports Stadium—Arlington, Texas

Esports are rapidly growing and changing. One constant will be the need for managers to plan and execute events from all levels, namely, publishers, games, teams, events, and venues.

This is a long list but still not an exhaustive one. Although there is not a lot of opportunity with any one team, one sport, or one league, there is quite a lot of opportunity in the cumulative. When it comes to internships, just because an organization does not post an opening does not mean they are unwilling to accept an intern's help. Do not be afraid to create your own opportunity.

While this list is in no way inclusive of every professional sport entity there is, it is meant to show you that there is much more to the world of professional sport than just a few "major league" franchises. Each of these entities can offer opportunities for students who are willing to go "outside the box" to find their futures.

- International Govern-
  ing Bodies – these are
  the organizations that
  have regulatory and
  sanctioning power over
  their sport internation-
  ally. These can also be
  the governing body of a
  group of competitions,
  like the International
  Olympic Committee
  for the Olympic Games.
  There are hundreds
  of such governing bodies, and just about every sport in the world
  has one from air sports (including aerobatics, air racing, ballooning,
  gliding, hang gliding, and parachuting/skydiving): Fédération Aéro-

nautique Internationale (FAI) to Yoga: Yogasports Confederation of World (YCW) and Elephant Polo: World Elephant Polo Association (WEPF) to Rubik's Cube: World Cube Association (WCA). Basically, anything that can be competed in has a governing body. These bodies offer opportunity to the student to learn about the governance of sport as well as the business involved.

- National Governing Bodies – these are the organizations that have control over a sport in a particular country. In the U.S. these bodies create and oversee our national teams as well. Again, there is a U.S. national governing body for just about any sport you can imagine playing, and national governing bodies present an enormous, and highly competitive, opportunity for students via internships. A quick internet search will get you to the sport of your choice.

- Collegiate Athletics – college athletics offers a large variety of opportunities for a student to work in sport in a number of different capacities. There are well over 500,000 student athletes participating at every level of collegiate athletics. There are approximately 1800 athletic departments in the NCAA, NAIA, and NJCAA. This represents a great deal of opportunity for those who wish to work in college athletics.

- Scholastic Sports – as budgets increase and more students are participating at the high school, and even middle school, level, the need for those who truly understand the business of sport will increase. Many school districts are consolidating athletic departments at the district level and hiring those with professional experience to run the operation. This is certainly a growth area. Another area of opportunity is private schools—from your small local school to large organizations specializing in the education of elite athletes, IMG Academies as an example. These types of organizations may not have the same teaching requirements that many public school systems have for their athletic department personnel and they still have the same functional needs as larger organizations.

- Amateur/Recreational Sport – today the line between recreational leagues and small professional organizations is a little blurred. Everywhere you turn there are academies for different sports with multiple, age-limited, travel teams. Even true recreational leagues have become big business. Just have a look at the Little League World Series. Organizations like the YMCA also offer sport programing and have staff to run the business of those offerings. Whether it is at the local, national, or international level, there is opportunity here.

This is a long list but still not an exhaustive one. While there is not a lot of opportunity with any one team, one sport, or one league, there is quite a lot of opportunity in the cumulative field. When it comes to internships, just because an organization does not post an opening, it does not mean they are unwilling to accept an intern's help. Do not be afraid to create your own opportunity.

ENTERTAINMENT

So, what is entertainment? It comes in all shapes and sizes. For the purposes of this book we will look at entertainment as live entertainment or, as it is also known, show business. According to the state of Nevada (Nevada Revised Statute (NRS) Chapter 368A -Tax on Live Entertainment; and Nevada Administrative Code (NAC) Chapter 368A), for tax purposes:

Live Entertainment is defined by statute as meaning any activity provided for pleasure, enjoyment, recreation, relaxation, diversion or other similar purpose by a person or persons who are physically present when providing an activity to a patron or group of patrons who are physically present.

It can include:

- *Music or vocals provided by one or more professional or amateur musicians or vocalists;*
- *Dancing performed by one or more professional or amateur dancers or performers;*
- *Acting or drama provided by one or more professional or amateur actors or players;*

- *Acrobatics or stunts provided by one or more professional or amateur acrobats, performers or stunt persons;*
- *Animal stunts or performances induced by one or more animal handlers or trainers, except animal behaviors induced by animal trainers or caretakers primarily for the purpose of education and scientific research;*
- *Athletic or sporting contests, events or exhibitions provided by one or more professional or amateur athletes or sportsmen except an athletic contest event or exhibition conducted by a professional team based in this State if the professional team based in this State is a participant in the contest, event or exhibition.*
- *Comedy or magic provided by one or more professional or amateur comedians, magicians, illusionists, entertainers or performers.*
- *A show or production involving any combination of the activities described above.*
- *A performance by a disc jockey who presents recorded music.*

This is as accurate as any definition and shows the wide variety of experiences you can find; but note that it does not include the recorded music industry. The music recording industry is very symbiotic with live music and should be included. If this definition is taken section by section, and recorded music is included, you can see the types of entities within each.

- Music – in all forms. The music industry includes composers (songwriters), recording, live music (concerts), artist management, and distribution. An entire book could be, and has been more than once, written on the music industry. There are entire programs devoted to just this part of the industry. This section will also include every genre of music from Blues to Hip Hop, Classical to Bluegrass, Rock to Reggae, and EDM to Pop music. Some of the entities and jobs available, aside from composers and performers, in this field include:
  - Producer – guides the production of a recording
  - Recording Engineer – operates and sets up recording equipment

© Amitofo/Shutterstock.com

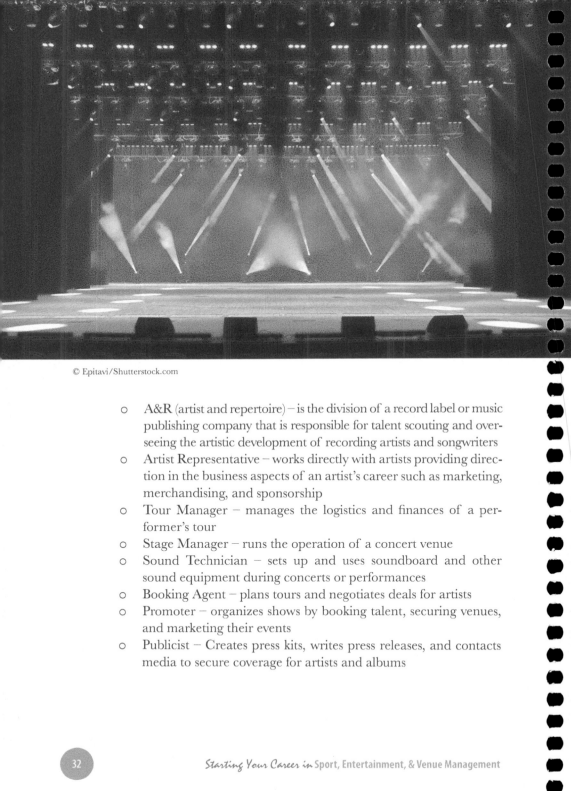

© Epitavi/Shutterstock.com

- o   A&R (artist and repertoire) – is the division of a record label or music publishing company that is responsible for talent scouting and overseeing the artistic development of recording artists and songwriters
- o   Artist Representative – works directly with artists providing direction in the business aspects of an artist's career such as marketing, merchandising, and sponsorship
- o   Tour Manager – manages the logistics and finances of a performer's tour
- o   Stage Manager – runs the operation of a concert venue
- o   Sound Technician – sets up and uses soundboard and other sound equipment during concerts or performances
- o   Booking Agent – plans tours and negotiates deals for artists
- o   Promoter – organizes shows by booking talent, securing venues, and marketing their events
- o   Publicist – Creates press kits, writes press releases, and contacts media to secure coverage for artists and albums

While not every entity will have all these types of positions, for any music act all are needed at some point. In many instances individuals, and organizations, may wear more than one hat. Some of the organizations where you can find these types of positions include:

© Marko Poplasen/Shutterstock.com

o   Sony Music
o   Warner Music
o   Virgin Records
o   Atlantic Records
o   Def Jam Records
o   Live Nation
o   AEG Live
o   OCESA/CIE
o   Messina Touring Group
o   Semmel Concerts Entertainment

This list is not close to inclusive of all the music-related organizations in the U.S. There are over 1000 record labels in the U.S. alone. There are thousands of promoters as well. Another avenue is music festivals. Again, these entities will have many of the same functions as above. Some of the larger organizations include:

o   AEG Presents
o   Outback Concerts
o   Broadway Entertainment Group Inc.
o   C3 Presents
o   Concert Republic
o   Nederlander Concerts

Again, these are not exhaustive lists. Today's live-music entertainment industry is very fluid, with multiple mergers, acquisitions, and sell-offs. The student should, and in Chapter 7 will, research the industry and organizations in which they wish to work.

• Live Shows – live shows are another widely varied area. These shows have the same functional areas and many of the same positions as music organizations. A live show is really anything people might want

© Doubleclix/Shutterstock.com

to come watch or buy a ticket to attend. With music covered in the last section, live shows include (with examples):

o Airshows – Heart of Texas Airshow, Thunder over Louisville
o Circus – Royal Hanneford Circus, Cirque Du Soleil
o Comedy – Stand-up Comedy - George Lopez, Ron White, Kevin Hart, Wanda Sikes
o Dance Shows – Riverdance, Lord of the Dance
o Family Shows – Feld Entertainment's Marvel Universe and Sesame Street Live
o Ice Shows – Disney on Ice (multiple touring shows)
o Magic – Masters of Illusion, Penn and Teller
o Performing Arts – Opera, Symphony

• Athletic or Sport Shows – we have already covered sport but there is a crossover component. While no one should argue that wrestlers are not athletic, it is very debatable whether professional wrestling is a sport. One thing that is certain is that it is entertaining and has a loyal following. Feld Motorsports does an incredible job of combining motorsports and entertainment as well.

o The Superstars of Gymnastics – featuring International Gymnastics Champions
o Stars on Ice – current and former ice-skating champions
o Harlem Globetrotters
o Monster Jam – Feld Entertainment Monster Truck Series
o Monster Energy Supercross – Feld Entertainment

o   Wrestling – WWE is a worldwide promotion and there are a number of national and regional promotions as well

VENUE

Merriam-Webster defines a venue as "a place where events of a specific type are held." That simple definition could not be more accurate and covers everything from a dairy farm in the Catskill Mountains of New York (Woodstock), seven square miles of Nevada's Black Rock Desert (Burning Man), or 900 acres in the Vale of Avalon (Glastonbury Festival) to iconic structures like the 20,000+ seat Madison Square Garden, the 90,000 seat Wembley Stadium, or the 100,000 seat Melbourne Cricket Grounds. A venue could be your backyard or the theatre onboard a cruise ship. Uniting each of these locations are very similar functional areas (covered in Chapter 7), and moving from one type to another during your career is quite possible.

- Racetrack – while there are multiple types of racing—horses, cars, trucks, motorcycles, and about any other contraption humans have learned to race—these facilities are also used for other purposes such as festivals and concerts. A few examples are:
  o   Watkins Glen, New York
  o   Circuit of the Americas, Texas
  o   Nürburgring, Germany
  o   Sydney Motorsport Park, Australia
  o   Churchill Downs, Kentucky
  o   Flemington Racecourse, Australia

© jamesteohart/Shutterstock.com

The streets of a city can also be used as a racetrack:

- o Surfers Paradise Street Circuit, Australia
- o Monaco Grand Prix, Monaco
- o Long Beach Grand Prix, California

- Conference and Convention Centers – come in all shapes and sizes and can be found in just about every metropolitan location.
  - o Dubai International Convention and Exhibition Center, Dubai
  - o Orange County Convention Center, Florida
  - o San Diego Convention Center, California
  - o Vancouver Convention Center, Canada
  - o Georgia World Congress Center, Georgia

- Outdoor Venues – will range from that dairy farm in New York to the Hollywood Bowl in Los Angeles, California to Augusta National Golf Course. Other examples include:
  - o Gorge Amphitheatre, Washington
  - o Fort Punta Christo, Croatia
  - o Wagner Park, Colorado
  - o Red Rocks Park and Amphitheatre, Colorado
  - o PNC Music Pavilion, North Carolina
  - o The Old Course, Scotland
  - o Pebble Beach Golf Links, California
  - o Bethpage Black Course, New York

- Theatres – are very flexible venues and allow for a range of events like Broadway shows, concerts, awards shows, and revues. A few examples include:
  - o Radio City Music Hall
  - o Belasco Theatre
  - o Tampa Theatre
  - o Sydney Opera House
  - o The Seebühne, Lake Constance, Austria
  - o Odeon of Herodes Atticus, Athens, Greece
  - o Palacio de Bellas Artes, Mexico City, Mexico

© Stephanie A Sellers/Shutterstock.com

© christian_b/Shutterstock.com

- Arenas and Stadiums – typically, in the U.S., have a resident professional or university team or teams. Their capacity can vary in size from a few thousand to well over 100,000. Stadiums may be open air, have retractable roofs, or have complete domes.
  o   AT&T Stadium, Dallas
  o   O2 Arena, London
  o   Stade Roland Garros, Paris
  o   Louisiana Superdome, New Orleans

© Ulrike Stein/Shutterstock.com

- o Wrigley Field, Chicago
- o Estadio Azteca, Mexico City
- o Philips Arena, Atlanta
- o Staples Center, Los Angeles
- o Allianz Arena, Munich

Again, a venue is any area or structure where an event can be hosted. The list above is meant only to show the student the wide variety of structures, entities, and organizations that can constitute a venue.

OUTSOURCED SERVICES

There is another avenue for the student to enter the sport, entertainment, and venue management world: outsourced services. For many of the functional areas of an organization there is the ability to allow another organization to provide the service. Much of this information, public versus private venue management and in-house versus outsourced services, will be covered in a sport, entertainment, and venue management program. Listed below are some examples of the types of services and the organizations who provide those services.

- Ticket Sales – many organizations contract with other organizations to deal with their ticket sales needs. Some of these other organizations may provide fan-to-fan ticket exchanges.
  - o The Aspire Group
  - o Learfield IMG College Ticket & Seat Solutions
  - o StubHub
  - o Ticketmaster

- Housekeeping and Cleaning Services
  - o ABM
  - o Anago Cleaning Systems
  - o JNS Commercial Cleaning
  - o Clean Event

- Crowd Management – organizations in this area may also offer services in security, ushering, ticket taking, guest services, and parking.
  - o Contemporary Services Corporation
  - o Crowd Management Services

- o Show Pros
- o Andy Frain Services

- Food Services and Hospitality
  - o Levy Restaurants
  - o Centerplate
  - o Sodexo
  - o Delaware North

- Marketing and Media
  - o GMR Marketing
  - o IMG
  - o Octagon
  - o MKTG
  - o Wasserman Media Group

- Venue Management – some venues, whether owned publicly or privately, may choose to engage a private management firm to oversee the operation of the facility. This can include operating the entire facility and all functional areas or only specifically contracted areas like those listed above and other areas such as booking, branding, and media.
  - o Spectra
  - o SMG
  - o VenuWorks
  - o Oak View Group
  - o AEG Facilities

- Event Management and Logistics – specialty companies that can create and execute events. They can be local event planners to international corporations. The jobs may range from a local corporate event to helping stage an Olympic Games. Some larger examples are:
  - o Incognitus
  - o Enterprise Events Group
  - o Global Experience Specialists
  - o Absolute Production Services

AGENCY

Being an agent can mean many different things to many different people and there are several agencies that span the entire spectrum of the industry. Some of the largest agencies are:

- Creative Artist Agency (CAA)
- Wasserman Media Group
- Excel Sports Management
- Octagon
- Boras Corporation
- Gestifute International
- Independent Sport and Entertainment
- Stellar Group
- Newport Sports Management
- Mino Raiola S.P.
- Legardere Sports
- WME-IMG

While this mass of information may seem overwhelming to a student trying to find their place in the industry, it really should be encouraging. It is also meant to show you all the opportunity in the industry if you are willing to be open-minded about different experiences. The most popular sports and franchises have, relatively, few employees and are incredibly popular with the average student. Being open to the different avenues available can still get you to the place you want to be.

CHAPTER 5

Defined Experiences

Every employer wants experience, but where do you get it, especially as a college student taking a full load of classes? The answer is simple, anywhere you can. Most organizations in the industry will want to see some type of experience and there are many different ways to get. Some experiences will be similar to what you wish to do in your career and some will not. All of it will be relevant. At times it can be difficult to understand how volunteering at a local 5K road race can get you a job in the NFL—but it can. There are many different kinds of experiences that can be used to gain experience and build your resume.

SHORT-TERM VOLUNTEER OPPORTUNITIES

Short-term volunteer opportunities are experiences that will last only a very defined period of time, a day, a weekend, a week-long event, and, most likely, be the student's first foray in the sport, entertainment, and venue industry. It is the quickest and easiest way for a student to begin to accumulate the experience hirers are looking for. It is also critical for the student to understand that, while they may not be interested in

the specific event at which they are volunteering, the act of volunteering itself shows a desire to be involved and learn. This has a value all its own.

These short-term opportunities can be found in numerous places. Perhaps your institution has an athletic department that regularly holds events. Maybe there is a music festival, or some other type of festival, in your town. Is there a PGA tour event nearby or a 5K road race that needs help? While students will have to balance academic responsibilities with volunteering, it is critical that they get involved. Take on as many opportunities as you can in as many different types of roles as possible. This will improve your overall sense of the industry, and your understanding of the hours required in this industry and your ability to handle them. You may be able to add other skills, like organization and customer service, which will look great on a resume. Perhaps, if you are lucky, even some leadership skills.

Your program or institution may have resources to inform you of these types of opportunities. Do not be afraid to ask for help locating them or reaching out to people who may need assistance. Often organizations do not think about a need they may have until someone asks. Get started as soon as you can and be involved. These will be the resume starters that lead to the next opportunities, long-term volunteer experiences. They also can be great fun.

LONG-TERM VOLUNTEER AND PART-TIME OPPORTUNITIES

You now have a few short-term experiences and, hopefully, have built a reputation as someone willing to jump in and help. Someone not afraid of long

© zhu difeng/Shutterstock.com

hours and hard work. It could be as simple as you have worked with your athletics marketing department a number of times and now they need someone to work a few hours a week in the office on an on-going basis. Office help is a great way to earn more time. Again, there needs to be a balance with academic responsibilities, so be honest, with the employer and yourself, with the amount of time you can allot to these opportunities.

These opportunities can also be money makers. Part-time jobs as ticket sellers in a local venue or a part-time worker in the operations department doing changeovers are examples of paying jobs. Perhaps it is working as an usher for a local minor league team. These jobs may not be in positions or with organizations you ultimately wish to work with they but can be resume items and earn you a little cash. They also will provide you with networking opportunities and a chance to showcase your abilities and work ethic.

Some places to look (but certainly not an exhaustive list):

- Your institution's athletic department
- Venues, stadiums, arenas, music venues, performing arts facilities
- Professional teams

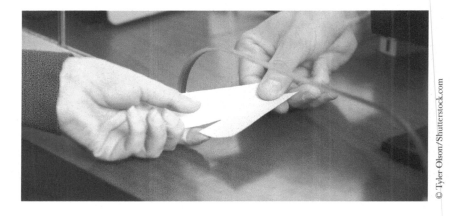

© Tyler Olson/Shutterstock.com

- Sports academies or other amateur sports organizations
- High school athletic departments, both public and private
- Golf courses
- Local sports commission or visitor's bureau in charge of bringing events to your locale
- Any organization responsible for the operation of a festival or other local celebration

While many of these opportunities may be counted as for-credit internships by your institution or program, for the purposes of this book, and the learning assignments, they are not considered full-time internships. They are still incredibly valuable to the student and their growth as an industry professional. They should be taken seriously and treated like a job interview. Give your best every day and do all you can to make a great impression.

FULL-TIME INTERNSHIPS

You have done all the preliminary work. You have put what you learned in the classroom to good use in both short- and long-term volunteer opportunities. Now it is time to step up your game. Full-time internships are just that, full-time. These will typically involve working full-time over an entire semester, or even an entire season or year, and involve more responsibility than your shorter-term experiences. Depending on the organization, they may be in one department or involve a rotational program for the student to see all aspects of how an organization runs.

For many organizations this is the entry-level position from which they promote. A long-term internship truly can be the student's opportunity to make an impression on an organization they want to work for. It is not unheard of for an organization to not only hire from their pool of interns but for the organization to hold a position for a prized intern until that student has completed their academic work, sometimes a year or more.

For the student this is truly the make or break time in their future career choice. You have heard your professors speak of long hours and hard, sometimes thankless, work. You cannot truly appreciate what that means until you experience it. This is your chance. It will be exciting, difficult, and fun, sometimes in the same day. Embrace the opportunity.

CHAPTER 6

Finding Your Passion

I remember growing up in Pittsburgh. My dad was a huge sports fan and he would take me to Steelers games and Penguin games. We would watch the Pirates on TV. One of the best days of my life was getting to go on the field before a Steelers' game and meeting several players. I was in awe. As I grew older I started playing sports, dreaming of being on the field with children looking up to me like I did to them. I loved to play all the sports but was really good at baseball. I had visions of playing at PNC Park! Eventually, like most athletes, I had to realize my playing days were over and I would not reach the pinnacle of the sport. I did know, however, that I wanted to stay involved in a sport and with a team I am so passionate about. I love all the Pittsburgh teams and really want to work for one of them someday.

Growing up, my parents always had music playing in the house. I remember being little and singing along into my hairbrush to my favorite songs. I became passionate about music and even played in a band in high school. We were not very good but I grew to love trying to book us gigs and making arrangements for our shows, even if they were only birthday parties, amateur nights at a local venue, or school talent shows. My passion for music has led me to what I want to do now. I want to be a tour manager for my favorite band. They are an

© dotshock/Shutterstock.com

up-and-coming group from my hometown but *I know they will make it big. I am just really passionate about helping them make it.*

I always remember playing travel baseball growing up. I lived to play. As I got older I only got better. I was lucky enough to win a state championship with my high school team my junior year. Unfortunately my senior year ended early with an injury that required surgery and my playing days were over just like that. I am so passionate about being at the field and around the players though that I believe I would love to work in baseball in the front office. I would be a great General Manager for my favorite team and we know they need one! My drive and passion for them would make us great.

Growing up in central Illinois, most us were either a Cardinals fan or a Cubs fan. One of the former, I would listen to Hall of Famer Jack Buck on my radio at night. I could picture Ozzie Smith, Vince Coleman, and Willie McGee playing as if they were in my backyard. I wanted to be the Cardinals play-by-play announcer someday. To go out to the ballpark every day and call the names of my childhood heroes was my dream job. What could be better than working for my favorite team!

© Ramona Kaulitzki/Shutterstock.com

Can you identify with any of these stories? Do you see yourself backstage as the tour manager of your favorite band or sitting in the dugout with the championship baseball team you assembled?

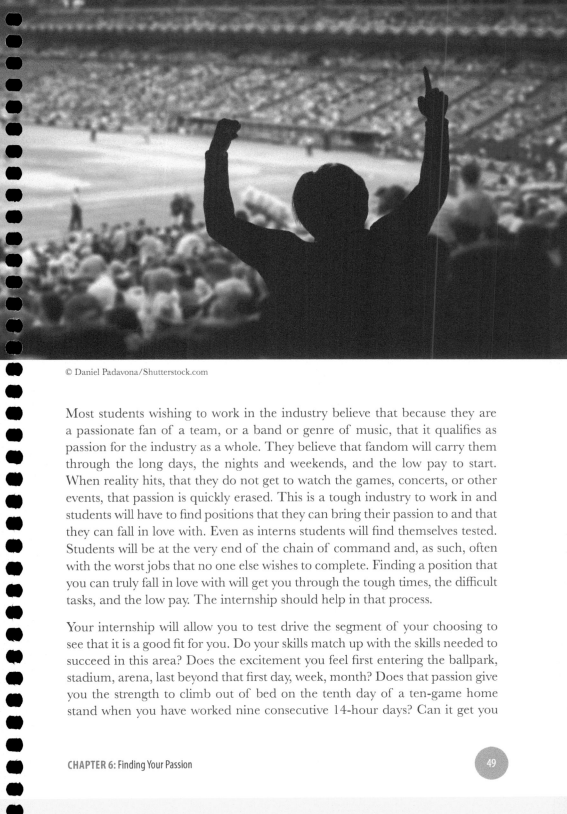

© Daniel Padavona/Shutterstock.com

Most students wishing to work in the industry believe that because they are a passionate fan of a team, or a band or genre of music, that it qualifies as passion for the industry as a whole. They believe that fandom will carry them through the long days, the nights and weekends, and the low pay to start. When reality hits, that they do not get to watch the games, concerts, or other events, that passion is quickly erased. This is a tough industry to work in and students will have to find positions that they can bring their passion to and that they can fall in love with. Even as interns students will find themselves tested. Students will be at the very end of the chain of command and, as such, often with the worst jobs that no one else wishes to complete. Finding a position that you can truly fall in love with will get you through the tough times, the difficult tasks, and the low pay. The internship should help in that process.

Your internship will allow you to test drive the segment of your choosing to see that it is a good fit for you. Do your skills match up with the skills needed to succeed in this area? Does the excitement you feel first entering the ballpark, stadium, arena, last beyond that first day, week, month? Does that passion give you the strength to climb out of bed on the tenth day of a ten-game home stand when you have worked nine consecutive 14-hour days? Can it get you

out of bed for an 8:00 am changeover in your arena when the night before you did not leave until after the 2:00 am settlement in the box office? Will it get you over the failure of your great idea (because this will most definitely happen) and give you the strength to try again?

This industry is about providing experiences to others, not for ourselves, and that is what the student must bring their passion to. How do you know you have the passion for the job? It is not something that will happen immediately, but as you work through your internship you should notice changes. The tasks may get tedious and you may not be excited about your colleagues but are you still excited to go into the office? That is a great start. You will really know you have made the switch when the people who paid to see your product matter as much or more than the product itself. Here are some examples:

Example 1: You are standing in front of the stage in your arena. The house lights go down and the crowd goes crazy. When the band begins to play the energy goes up even higher. You are excited and feeding off the crowd's energy because you know you helped make this happen. It is about those people in front of you who bought the tickets and the act behind you is, almost, irrelevant.

Example 2: You are working as a marketing intern for a traveling family show and you are shadowing at a performance. As you move about the arena you see a seven or eight-year-old child with eyes as big as saucers because she has just seen her favorite princess skate by. This little one is living a dream and you helped make it happen. It really does not matter which princess, or even if it is a princess, all that matters is that that child is having the time of her life.

Example 3: You are a community relations intern for that Pittsburgh NFL team and you are in charge of the meet-and-greet before the game. You are escorting a family with a child in a wheelchair onto the sidelines pregame and you introduce them to that child's favorite player. It is your favorite player too, one you idolized when you were a small child, but that is unimportant right now as you see the reaction of the child in the wheelchair. You know that child has a memory that will last a lifetime and you assisted in making it happen.

There are many more examples like these. This industry provides moments for others. As an industry professional that is what you will do. When you find yourself truly passionate about the job and not the team or the band or the show you will have the energy it takes for a career in the sport, entertainment, and venue industry. At some point in your career, it may be in your internship(s) or in your first job, you should have a moment, an A-HA moment, when everything becomes clear that this is the industry for you. It will be different for everyone, and it may be a series of moments, but you will know when it does happen. If this does not happen for you, if you are still more awed by meeting a player or a singer, then a change of career choices may be a good idea.

© Brocreative/Shutterstock.com

> "The sports industry is a small, tight-knit community — put your best foot forward (personality-wise and work product) with everyone you meet. Your reputation will always precede you, and the chances are whoever is hiring for your next opportunity knows someone who knows you."
>
> *Myles B. Solomon • Director - Coaches Division • Element Sports Group*

> On the importance of a great attitude, "It's number one. This industry is pretty small and a lot of people want to be in it, so if you have a bad attitude, you will get fired."
>
> *Stewart Blanchard • Assistant Tour Manager • Zac Brown Band*

SECTION 3

Preparing for the Internship Search

HELLO
I AM...

PREPARED

© iQoncept/Shutterstock.com

Finding your place in any industry can be a daunting task. Trying to decide on a direction in an industry with so many different avenues can be overwhelming. Add to this the competitive nature of the business and it might be easy to get lost. Preparing for your internship search, and your future career, can be of great value to you going forward. Researching what jobs are out there and what they entail is important. Understanding the law and what it means to you as an intern is equally so. What is going on in your life can have a bearing on where and when you apply. Once those decisions are made you need to put your best foot forward in applying, as the industry is incredibly competitive. This section will walk you through how to research positions, recognize factors that can affect your choices, and prepare you to apply and win the right internship.

CHAPTER 7

Researching an Industry Segment

Earlier, the various industries—sport, entertainment, venues, etc.—were defined, but just saying that you want to work in, say, sport will not get you where you want to be. Also, as discussed earlier, you must find something you can be passionate about, something that will keep you moving forward in the middle of a ten-game home stand or after a five-night run at your venue.

There are many different avenues a student can follow, and most are interconnected, or can, at the very least, provide transferable skills, but how do you learn about working the job? Your classes and professors will assist you in learning about the industry. You can use the internet as there are many articles on working in the industry and you can use

© Polly Grimm/Shutterstock.com

job hunting websites as well. While job descriptions can give you a general idea of what the job may entail, a general idea is just that—general. Descriptions often fall well short of all working in this industry means. The best way to learn about working in the industry, however, is to go to the source. Interviewing those who do the job not only gives the student the best, most up to date information, it allows them to begin to develop a network of their own and industry mentors.

To provide more focus to the topic of the research, a specific area of the industry can be selected. Some areas, although not an exhaustive list, include:

- Ticket operations
- Sales
  o Ticket
  o Sponsorship
  o VIP and suite
  o Advertising
- Marketing
- Team operations
- Venue operations
- Community outreach
- Public relations
- Event management
- Agency
  o Player representation
  o Act (band, singer, show) representation
  o Sponsor representation
- Analytics
- Finance
- Accounting
- Athletic departments
  o Collegiate
  o High school
- Tour management
- Promoter
  o Concert
  o Family show
  o Sporting event
- Guest services
- Event security

Once you have selected the area you need to find people to speak with. Doing this research, speaking with industry professionals in a chosen area, will be time consuming; these folks are busy with their jobs. One thing most of them have in common, however, is their willingness to speak with students about their industries. Most of the contacts you will speak with have been where you are now and will be willing to help. There are a number of ways to reach sources in the industry. For starters, your professors may have contacts to share with you or perhaps a classmate. There may be a means for you to reach alumni of your program who work in the industry as well. Ask everyone involved in your program. Next, it is time to start locating individuals who do the job. Finding contact information can be difficult but team and/or organization websites are a place to start. Many will not have listings for staff members but general contact numbers and email addresses. The phone can be a great tool. The phone book will often have a local number listed for an organization but when you call you must be prepared to ask for the person you wish to speak with by name. Rarely will the person answer but you may reach their voicemail. If you do not know who the person you wish to speak to is, it is unlikely you will get anywhere. Professional networking sites like LinkedIn can be a resource for the student to reach potential sources. Job postings may contain contact information as well. As you reach the first few people it may be possible to reach others through them. Do not be afraid to ask. You should use at least three sources, but the more you have the better your information and evaluation will be.

The next question is, "what do I (the student) want to ask?" As you are learning about the positions you should also be evaluating the career path. There are some basic questions everyone should ask for any of the positions listed above. They are:

- What are the typical tasks required of an entry-level person in this field?
- What skills and qualifications do I need to be successful?
- What types of hours would this person work? Nights? Weekends? Holidays?
- What would an entry-level salary look like for someone just starting out? (This number will vary wildly based on locations and organizations.)
- Are there jobs available? Where?

The next set of questions will be more personal to the person doing the research. What is important to you? Some samples are:

- What does a typical career path look like?
- Is there opportunity for growth? Rapid growth?
- What makes the job rewarding?
- What is one thing you wish you had known before starting this job?
- How has the job changed in recent years and where is it headed?
- How does this career impact lifestyle? For example, travel, late nights, family, etc.
- What classes should I take to make me more valuable to an organization, especially elective classes?
- What makes a new employee stand out?

You may also choose to ask more personal questions such as:

- Knowing what you know now, would you still choose to pursue a career in…?
- If you could give yourself one piece of advice before entering this field what would it be?
- What do you enjoy most working in this industry? Least?

The above lists are not exhaustive and many of the questions will be up to the researcher. The most important question is one you should ask yourself. What do I want to know? Make sure you prepare enough questions to get that answer.

You have your list of contacts now (a list that can and will evolve as you go) and your questions. Now it is time to reach out to them. You do not want to just cold-email a list of questions to a list of names you know nothing about. Remember that part of this research is creating relationships with those who work in the industry. It is critical to your success that you present yourself in a professional manner and behave accordingly. You will have many options in how you reach out to your sources, including phone, email, and social media. Making contact should be a several-step process.

1. Making initial contact – initial contact should involve who you are and what you are trying to accomplish. You are trying to create a relationship and gather the information you want. Again, be professional and understanding of the person's time. Be prepared for last-minute cancellations as these folks are doing the job and more pressing matters may arise. Do not take it personally. These people are busy and you want some of that valuable time. Conduct yourself accordingly. The outcome you want here is to set up a time to communicate directly with the source that is convenient for them. Ideally that would be in-person or via the phone; but that may not always be available, in which case and an email exchange of questions and answers can be used.

2. The interview – as stated above, in-person is the ideal way to conduct this interview. If you are lucky enough to have a sit-down with your source, remember to dress accordingly. It will never hurt you to make the best impression you can. If you conduct the interview over the phone, make sure you are in a position to not have the call dropped. Both in-person and on the phone will allow you to work on your oral communication skills as well. Be conscious of their time in all situations. Again, email is the least desirable way to get the information you want. It does not allow for any give and take or for you to create new questions based on answers in the moment. Again, make sure your emails are presented in a polite and professional manner. You want their help and you want to make a great impression.

3. Follow-up – you have your information—now what? Once the interview is conducted the first thing to do is to send a handwritten thank

you note. One more time, you are trying to expand your network and create relationships. Little can make a better impression than a handwritten note. You may also connect with them on a professional site such as LinkedIn. Compile your data and compare the answers from your different sources. This may lead to new questions for your sources as well.

4. Evaluation – is this career path for you? This is the most personal part of the research. At this point you have met with, and spoken to, a number of industry professionals. Do you see yourself in this position? Can you live with the hours, compensation, and impact on your personal life? Are you still excited about the idea of working in the industry? If yes, it is time to start looking for an internship. If no, during your interviews did you learn of another segment that fits your career goals better? Do you need to research other areas?

5. Continuation – growing the relationships you have created. During your interviews you learned about your sources and, potentially, found items in common. Perhaps you are from the same home state or the same college. Maybe you are fans of the same teams or acts. Those are things you can use as an excuse to communicate with that person again. Perhaps their organization won a big series or even a championship. Reach out and congratulate them. Find any reason to continue the conversation. When you do reach out to them again, especially if it has been a while, reply to an old email. This allows you to remind them who you are without having to remind them who you are.

Starting Your Career in Sport, Entertainment, & Venue Management

CHAPTER 8

Internships and the Law

Student learning in an internship will stem from knowledge and experiences specific to the setting, growth in interpersonal communication skills, and exposure to a professional workplace. It should include awareness of the legal issues inherent in internships. Students, institutions of higher learning and their representatives, and sites hosting interns should all be familiar with the legal landscape of internships, especially in these litigious times.

The legal areas relevant to internships include discrimination law, travel policies, and contract law. Students are encouraged to work with their institutional mentor to develop the necessary command of these topics. These topics are important but not the focus of this chapter. Neither are individual state or local laws. This chapter will focus on applicable federal legislation, specifically the Fair Labor Standards Act, and the concept of duty and how it and related terms are applicable to the sport business internship industry.

© MIND AND I/Shutterstock.com

DUTY

A duty is a responsibility to others to act according to law. A defendant being accused of a breach of duty must have some obligation imposed by law to protect a plaintiff from an unreasonable risk. This can be complex in a college setting where most students are adults.

NEGLIGENCE

The concept of duty owed surfaces in the definition of negligence. An institution or its representatives can be found negligent when their conduct involves an unreasonably great risk of causing damage and falls below the standard established by law for protection of others against unreasonable risk of harm. Negligence does not require or include an intent to cause injury or harm. An act of negligence could be an act of omission, failure to do something such as warning an intern of previous dangers involved with a particular agency, or an act of commission, the act of doing something inappropriately.

There are four things that must be proven in a negligence case:

- Established duty of care was owed to the plaintiff by the defendant
- The defendant breached that duty
- The breach of duty was a proximate cause of plaintiff's injuries
- The plaintiff suffered damages, which can be defined as an injury, loss, or deterioration caused by the negligence, design, or accident of one person to another in respect to the latter's person or property.

FORESEEABILITY

Foreseeability refers to the concept that the legal system expects trained professionals to foresee dangers and act accordingly. A game official who observes lightning would not allow a game or concert to continue because they can foresee the danger of a potential strike. Courts will expect interns to have the knowledge and experience to foresee certain dangers and are even more likely to hold their supervisors at their internship site and university accountable for such foreseeability.

ASSUMPTION OF RISK

A common defense against negligence claims involves the concept of assumption of risk. There are two types of assumption of risk – primary and secondary. Primary assumption of risk means that a plaintiff understands the risks of an activity and voluntarily agrees to accept the risks. This could involve the risks associated with driving to and from work, or the understanding that fans at a venue could be confrontational.

An important question must be raised. Can students truly voluntarily accept risks if an internship is a graduation requirement? Case history on this question pertaining to university physical education activity requirements are mixed, but a preponderance of the decisions would suggest the university has a greater duty surrounding their graduation requirements. So would the duty from either the academic institution (likely) or the agency (not as likely) be different if the student is receiving academic credit for the experience or not? What risks would the courts assume the "average intern" would know? Would sport management majors or students with previous experience in the sport business industry be held to a higher standard?

A second form is secondary assumption of risk, when a plaintiff "deliberately chooses to encounter a known risk and in doing so acts unreasonably." This could include an intern's own behavior leading to an injury, for example purposefully driving a golf cart too fast in a restricted area and crashing.

One notorious case helps shape light on some of these questions. Gross was a graduate student in psychology at Nova Southeastern University in Florida who was required to complete an eleven-month practicum. She was provided a list of approved places and was allowed to identify her top six choices before ultimately being assigned one by the university. The place where she was assigned, Family Services Agency Inc., was in a location known to have a higher concentration of criminal activity. University officials were aware of this fact.

Gross was accosted, robbed, and sexually assaulted one evening walking to her car after working at her internship. She sued Family Services Agency, where she eventually settled, and Nova Southeastern for negligence.

The school identified three issues in their defense.

- Gross was an adult and so a special relationship did not exist.
- The school did not owe Gross a duty to inform of dangers because she already knew them.
- The school not telling Gross about the dangers was not the proximate cause of the injury. (Nova Southeastern vs. Gross)

The courts ruled the university had a duty to make students aware of the foreseeable acts of a third party. The court acknowledged this duty is not the same as owed a child in elementary or secondary school, but indicated a relationship still exists. This was compounded by the fact that an internship was required and Nova ultimately decided the site. Thus, it is plausible that if Gross had selected the site and Nova merely approved it that the legal outcome might have been different.

FAIR LABOR STANDARDS ACT

The other legal area this chapter focuses on deals with relevant federal legislation, specifically the Fair Labor Standards Act (FLSA).

The Fair Labor Standards Act establishes minimum wage, overtime pay, recordkeeping, and child labor standards affecting full-time and part-time workers in the private sector and in federal, state, and local governments. It was originally drafted in 1938 in part to establish a federal minimum wage, provide for overtime pay after a 40-hour work-week, and to suppress nefarious child-labor practices.

This piece of legislation has a long history of governing unpaid internships. Past guidelines included a six-prong test offering guidance to interns and agencies hiring them. However, high-profile abuses in the entertainment industry have led to different guidelines.

The most recent changes to the law occurred in January 2018. This was at least in part a response to Wang vs. Hearst Corporation, where a magazine company prevailed against some of its unpaid interns. Interns were not being paid and alleged they were not receiving special guidance or supervision and were not assigned difficult tasks. The Second Circuit of Appeals, after acknowledging that not every person performing a service for a company legally constitutes an employee protected under the Fair Labor Standards Act, refuted their claims and ruled that the plaintiffs were receiving educational benefits and were the primary beneficiary and thus were not eligible for grievance under the FLSA. The Department of Labor adopted a fact sheet mirroring what was stated in the ruling. This sheet offered guidance to examine the economic reality of the intern-employer relationship and to determine the primary beneficiary. A seven-factor test was implemented and replaces the previous six-part test. A major change is that now not all factors need to be satisfied. The test is as follows:

THE TEST FOR UNPAID INTERNS AND STUDENTS

Courts have used the "primary beneficiary test" to determine whether an intern or student is, in fact, an employee under the FLSA. In short, this test allows courts to examine the "economic reality" of the intern-employer relationship to determine which party is the "primary beneficiary" of the relationship. Courts have identified the following seven factors as part of the test:

1.   The extent to which the intern and the employer clearly understand that there is no expectation of compensation. Any promise of compensation, express or implied, suggests that the intern is an employee—and vice versa.
2.   The extent to which the internship provides training that would be similar to that which would be given in an educational environment, including the clinical and other hands-on training provided by educational institutions.
3.   The extent to which the internship is tied to the intern's formal education program by integrated coursework or the receipt of academic credit.
4.   The extent to which the internship accommodates the intern's academic commitments by corresponding to the academic calendar.
5.   The extent to which the internship's duration is limited to the period in which the internship provides the intern with beneficial learning.
6.   The extent to which the intern's work complements, rather than displaces, the work of paid employees while providing significant educational benefits to the intern.
7.   The extent to which the intern and the employer understand that the internship is conducted without entitlement to a paid job at the conclusion of the internship.

Courts have described the "primary beneficiary test" as a flexible test, and no single factor is determinative. Accordingly, whether an intern or student is an employee under the FLSA necessarily depends on the unique circumstances of each case.

If analysis of these circumstances reveals that an intern or student is actually an employee, then he or she is entitled to both minimum wage and overtime pay under the FLSA. On the other hand, if the analysis confirms that the intern or student is not an employee, then he or she is not entitled to either minimum wage or overtime pay under the FLSA.

NOT FOR PROFITS

Still at issue could be the application of these federal guidelines to interns in the public sector or not-for-profit sector and not in the private for-profit business sector. Department of Labor regulations may allow these individuals to count as volunteers, especially if there is a "civic, charitable, or humanitarian purpose." A volunteer is defined by the FLSA as "an individual who performs hours of service for a public agency for civic, charitable, or humanitarian reasons, without promise, expectation, or receipt of compensation for services rendered." Courts have ruled that a student performing an internship for academic credit could negate the aforementioned claim.

SUMMARY

There are several legal issues applicable to student interns. Students, site supervisors, and institutional representatives should all familiarize themselves with different scenarios.

CHAPTER 9

Life Factors

Completing the internship will be an exciting time and afford you great career-enhancing opportunities. Yet there will be sacrifices and even obstacles to overcome to maximize the experience. These can include financial limitations, personal relationships, and competing priorities.

FINANCIAL LIMITATIONS

It is recognized that college students don't have money. This generalization can especially impact students during their internships, where they can face pressure on both sides of the balance sheet. Students may have to pay additional

© MariBa/Shutterstock.com

tuition costs for their internship while at the same time not receiving any compensation during the experience, a most likely scenario.

Chapter 8 discussed the legal circumstances concerning when an internship can be unpaid. But even those companies that do offer compensation rarely pay much, and certainly not enough for you to be able to adequately save when considering living expenses, clothes, social networking, outings, and other intangible expenses.

Your institution will have its own practices concerning internship charges. Some schools build the cost of an internship directly into tuition costs, especially when the experience is part of a traditional semester. Special fees may or may not be included in these instances. Other schools may charge you per the credit hour and yet others may charge a flat rate. Financial aid may or may not be available for internships and so you are encouraged to familiarize yourself with your own institutional practices.

Each of you has unique socioeconomic circumstances and sometimes the default opinion of some professors and industry practitioners that "you just have to find a way" isn't reassuring. Hopefully you are reading this book early enough in your academic career so that you and your family, if applicable, can do their best to plan ahead. Regardless of your timeline, you should be researching and projecting your expenses such as tuition, fees, and possible relocation costs. You should find ways to save money while you are working at jobs during summer, break periods, or the semester. You should have a strategy of saving for your internship similar to other important life purchases. This includes earning money and also avoiding spending when unnecessary.

It is important that you pursue your internship opportunity without having to take on a second job while at the internship, even if such a thing would be allowed. The second job often becomes the priority because it funds your living expenses. There is also the real possibility that it could detract from your

© Huahinstocker/Shutterstock.com

ability to get all you can from your internship. It can keep you from taking on extra tasks or shadowing key figures you may not directly work for outside your normal work hours. This type of scenario should be avoided if at all possible.

Part of your research includes asking your advisor, career office, or other appropriate individuals or offices what scholarships or programs your institution has specifically for internships. Examples of available scholarships could be dependent on your family income and whether you are completing an internship at a location outside of your hometown or your college's community. Your school may also have alumni who are willing to host students in their communities who are completing an internship, essentially affording you living expenses. The worst you can be told is that such programs don't exist.

Finally there are other ways to mitigate the expense through research. Where do you have friends and family who might be able to give you a place to stay? Creating a list of free or low cost locations will be highly beneficial. Once you have this research check for what organizations are available in those locales that would be of interest to you and apply for those that are appropriate.

> Scenario: You have been offered a great but unpaid internship during a summer semester. You don't have the $4,000 to cover tuition costs or much monies to offset living costs and the only available financial aid is loans. You already have accumulated close to $40,000 in student loan debt and have a full year of college left. You have also been offered a second-tier internship in your hometown, where you could live at home to avoid living expenses and work occasionally at your old job to make some money. What are your considerations?
>
> Meet with everyone you can to discuss the financial implications. Your program's internship director or other faculty member responsible for internships, your institution's financial aid office, your parents or other family who may be of assistance.
>
> Evaluate the experiential benefit of each internship. Can you gain the same experience and transferable skills? Is there a value to you in showing you can move away from home and be successful in a job? Can you create the same value in connections for your network? Will you be given the same level of responsibility?
>
> Complete a cost-benefit analysis. Does the "great" internship actually offer you more of the things you need to make it worth the extra cost? Does it make you significantly more valuable on the job market? Your mentors and/or a faculty member can assist in this process.

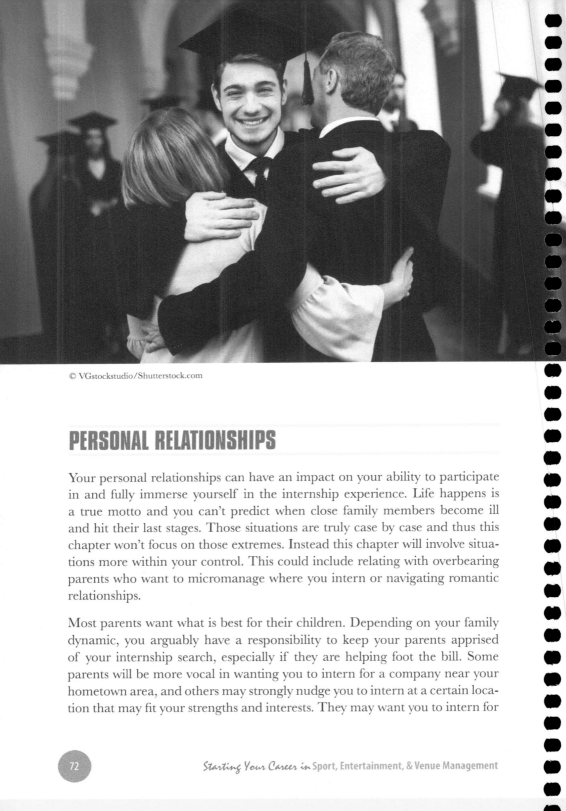

© VGstockstudio/Shutterstock.com

PERSONAL RELATIONSHIPS

Your personal relationships can have an impact on your ability to participate in and fully immerse yourself in the internship experience. Life happens is a true motto and you can't predict when close family members become ill and hit their last stages. Those situations are truly case by case and thus this chapter won't focus on those extremes. Instead this chapter will involve situations more within your control. This could include relating with overbearing parents who want to micromanage where you intern or navigating romantic relationships.

Most parents want what is best for their children. Depending on your family dynamic, you arguably have a responsibility to keep your parents apprised of your internship search, especially if they are helping foot the bill. Some parents will be more vocal in wanting you to intern for a company near your hometown area, and others may strongly nudge you to intern at a certain location that may fit your strengths and interests. They may want you to intern for a family business, but your institution may have rules curtailing this practice. You may also have family that guilt-trip you upon discovering you can't take the two-week family vacation this year because you can't ask for that time off. Family members will understand…or they won't. Accepting that each family dynamic is unique, you must be prepared to stand firm concerning your internship choices and your future. You will likely know the best strategies and how early you need to start your persuasion. Some talking points for these discussions are (and your faculty advisor or internship director may be able to assist with these as well):

- Explain the uniqueness of the industry and why this experiential learning is critical.
- Your internship is a long-term job interview in reality and it makes a bad impression to ask for time off during the short period of time an internship usually encompasses.
- Relate how the creation of relationships with industry professionals is critical to your future success and can only be created via the appropriate internships.

You may experience a similar dynamic with a romantic partner. Some readers are married and/or have children. This section's focus will be more on unmarried readers who are in a committed romantic relationship and are faced with the prospect of not being with them for a multi-month period of time. Insecurities may emerge on fidelity or growing apart. Not to use yet another cliché in this chapter, but it is true that if a relationship is meant to be then it will be. Hopefully you are with someone who can respect your need to be apart for a short time so you can advance your opportunities. Your relationship is unique and important to you, but most readers will be advised to make the short-term personal sacrifice for your career. However, you do have a responsibility as a caring partner to communicate with your significant other about your internship selection process.

Scenario: You have landed a great internship with a top entertainment venue five hours away. Your significant other wants to start looking for summer jobs in that same area so you can spend quality time together. You enjoy your relationship and definitely want to see this person when possible, but you are worried that if you are in the same town you will feel pressure to spend more time with them than you may have available. You want to make a positive impression at the internship. In the end every relationship dynamic is different but here are a few tips on how to approach the necessary conversation:

- Explain the uniqueness of the industry and why this experiential learning is critical. Also cover the long hours you will be expected to work.
- Once again, this is a long-term job interview and making the right impression will be very important. As such you will want to work as many hours as possible to make that favorable impression, leaving little time for yourself or anything else.
- Often explaining the importance of this opportunity to your future together can have a positive impact as well.

COMPETING PRIORITIES

You may have other priorities that make accepting an internship difficult. You may already have a job that pays well and for which you have developed a strong routine and a loyalty, and you are hesitant to leave them short-handed. You also may already have an internship with a firm in your campus community but your advisor is pushing you to take on a new experience. In both cases you are advised to accept something different. No disrespect is meant to our readers' abilities, but in most cases you are replaceable and your previous employer or internship site will be just fine provided you offer them acceptable notice. As with the financial considerations, it is critical you do what is best for your future in the industry. Does your current job actually give you the skills and connections you need to be successful?

Scenario: You attend a university in a small city with no professional sport franchises within an easy commuting distance. You have been working in the box office of your on-campus arena since your freshman year. You have been promoted to a supervisory role and given increasing responsibility since that time. There has also been talk of offering you a full-time position after graduation. You have a desire to work for a professional team and have earned an internship with an MLB team in their ticketing operations, your desired position. When you bring up the subject of the MLB position your boss seems hurt and angry by the possibility you may leave.

    o   The first question to ask yourself is, "where do I want to be in a few years?" While no career will follow a linear path and opportunities may come from the strangest of places, you have to be focused on a direction you are truly willing to work hard towards. If you are not willing to put forth your best effort then a change of direction is what is called for.

© Rocksweeper/Shutterstock.com

o   You know you have a good idea of where you want to go. Next evaluate the positions to determine which gives you the best chance to reach your destination. Making lists of the positives and negatives for each is a good start. Are you gaining the experience you need (i.e., transferable skills)? Do you have the ability to network? Is there room to grow?

o   Now you know where you are going and you have evaluated your options. Make a decision and stick with it. Handle yourself professionally and politely but make a choice. It is important to be respectful as you do not want to close any doors for yourself or burn any bridges. It is also important to understand that you cannot make a wrong choice if you are willing to work hard wherever you decide to go. If it is a place where you can give your best effort it will lead you where you want to go.

It is also possible you are a student-athlete and your coaches have high expectations on your time commitment to working out and staying active with team activities. You may be a fall athlete who may have to report in the fall to training camp, with such an early date making you unattractive as a candidate for a summer internship. In most cases, communication again is key. You should begin communicating with your coaches as soon as you have ideas. Don't assume your coaches know the required courses for every academic major your institution offers. This is also a time to be communicating with your academic advisor or other mentor. Your advisor or mentor may have to intervene on your behalf with the coaching staff, although each campus climate is different concerning the likely success of any such intervention. If you make a decision that you aren't going to be able to miss athletic commitments, then hopefully your coaches will allow you to complete smaller experiences, even if they are local or on-campus. Completing experiences during your off-season and after your eligibility is completed are other options. Your athletic department may also have a program to assist as well.

CONCLUSION

Hopefully this chapter and the scenarios have helped you identify the obstacles you may encounter when deciding to accept an internship. Certainly this chapter cannot identify each of them and everyone's situation is different. But regardless, communication with all constituents and effective planning will go a long way in helping you overcome them. The sooner you begin the process the greater the likelihood of a favorable outcome.

CHAPTER 10

Considering Where to Apply

I want to work for the Red Sox. I want to intern with the Bears. I want to work at Madison Square Garden. I want to intern with William Morris. Making your selection for where to apply for an internship may seem like a simple process. Just select your favorite team or entity and there you go. In the end it may not be that simple, but, with proper preparation, it does not have to be that difficult either. There are a number of questions you can ask yourself to sort out the best "where to apply" for you. Most students who make the decision to enter the industry do so, at first, with unrealistic expectations based on their fandom of, or participation in, a sport, a team, an act, or other entity. There are many critical decisions that must be made before the application process should be undertaken. Before you select the major sport franchise or leading agency or largest promoter or most iconic venue to make your application you should ask yourself a few questions. These include:

- Where can I live?
- Can I support myself financially?

- What can I get out of the experience?
- Where should I be?

Successfully navigating where to apply takes planning and it is best to begin as soon as possible. Waiting until the last minute to make some of the necessary arrangements may leave you with uninspiring options in internships that provide little of the learning you need to accomplish.

WHERE CAN I LIVE?

This simple question can really set the student up for more opportunity if answered thoroughly. Housing can be the biggest deterrent to obtaining a meaningful, productive internship. If that issue can be resolved much stress can be relieved and allow the student to focus on learning on the job. You want to be someplace you can be secure in your living arrangement and, preferably, somewhere you would not need a second job to support the first. So how is this accomplished? Make a list.

This is a time when family and friends can be of great benefit. Of course, you would include where your parents live but where are other family members you could reasonably ask for help? Family friends? Siblings? Once you compile this list, research what organizations are in those areas and evaluate them based on what you can get out of each experience.

© CC7/Shutterstock.com

If that list is too short or not productive enough there are other, low cost, options. Looking at university housing near a desired location is one option. Often institutions will have housing available at an affordable rate. Websites like studenthousing.org, campusrent.com, internhousing.com or mycheapa-partments.com can be a resource as well. An internet search can also be productive. Your program or institution may have an office that can help you find housing with alumni willing to host you in your internship area as well. Ask someone, as it may be an informal program. Again, once your list is made, evaluate the opportunities available in the chosen locales.

CAN I SUPPORT MYSELF FINANCIALLY?

An important part of the where question revolves around your ability to support yourself financially. There is a very good chance your internship will be unpaid or paid at a very low rate. That is just the reality of a highly competitive industry. If you are fortunate enough to get paid, that is a bonus, but you should not base your decision solely on getting paid. The experience, not a few dollars, will be what is most critical to your future career and its success. Again, planning will be critical, whether it is saving money to cover costs or finding ways, like free or inexpensive housing, to limit the financial impact.

There is also a chance that you will have to pay tuition if your internship is for credit. Some programs and institutions may have scholarships available to offset this cost so be sure to ask your internship coordinator or financial aid office. There are also national organizations that offer scholarships for students in certain industries, such as the Stadium Managers Association Student Scholarship, the National Golf Course Owners' Association Don Rossi Scholarship, and the Live Nation U.S. Concerts Scholarship Program. An internet search can provide opportunities for funding.

You will need to be honest and realistic with yourself about what your budget can manage. While you have the option of taking a second job to fund your internship this is not an ideal situation for a number of reasons. You are going to work long hours during your internship. Adding a second job will only amplify the stress on you physically. A tired intern is probably not a learning intern. The second job has the potential to overtake the internship in importance because it is what is supporting you financially. Is it possible that you might take time off from the internship in order to take an extra shift at your second job?

© Mascha Tace/Shutterstock.com

Would you pass on an extra opportunity at your internship because you need an extra shift at the paying job?

These examples are a real risk if you need that paying job and can be detrimental not only to the internship but also to your career progression. Your internship is an extended job interview and you really want your focus to be on it solely. You do not want to leave a bad impression on your internship employer.

WHAT CAN I GET OUT OF THE EXPERIENCE?

You have your list of locations and know you can support yourself financially. Now come perhaps the most important questions, and this is not an exhaustive list.

- What are my career aspirations and how does this internship fit into them?
- What do I want to get out of my internship?
- Do I want to turn this into a full-time employment opportunity?
- Do I want a "major league" experience or is a smaller organization better suited to me?
- Can I gain the skills I need to be successful in my career?
- Do I want to focus in one area (because I know what I want) or do I want something that is rotational (so I can see all aspects)?

- Will I be able to work on real projects or are "intern" jobs all I will experience?
- Do I want to expand my network greatly or is one or two additions enough?
- Will I have access to contacts in other departments to expand my network?

Depending on where you are in your academic career the answers will vary. Younger students' career aspirations are only beginning to evolve, whereas a senior should, by this time, have a good idea of a direction. Each student will have a different set of needs and wants from their internship experience and it is a good idea to discuss what yours are with a faculty, or other, mentor. A rising junior is not necessarily ready to accept a full-time offer, so the potential for full-time employment is not as important to a junior as it would be to a graduating senior.

© Rawpixel.com/Shutterstock.com

Many students become consumed with the "major league" opportunities, whether they be with a team, a large named corporation, or other iconic organization. It is important to realize these are the most popular and, thus, the most competitive, but also to ask if the major league experience is truly necessary. The summer collegiate wood bat league team still requires all the functional areas, such as game operations, marketing, community relations, and ticket sales, as an NFL franchise so the skills you acquire will be the same. If you can market a baseball game, you can market a concert or a family show or an arena football team.

Organizations of all sizes may have rotational internships. These allow a student to see many different functional areas during the course of the internship. Each will vary in length and functional areas included depending on the organization and their needs. These rotational internships are a good chance for someone new to the industry to get a feel for every type of job available. They also allow for the student to be exposed to many different staff with the host organization, and thus rotational internships lend themselves to building a network.

Whereas a large organization like the NFL franchise may have 100 plus employees, the summer collegiate wood bat league team may have four or five full-time employees. Smaller organizations can, potentially, provide the student with greater opportunity for learning as they tend to have smaller staffs. They need more help and it is typically an all-hands-on-deck type of attitude when it comes to getting things done. Students may also have a greater chance of working on meaningful, long-term projects and have the ability to use their creativity. More than one career professional in the industry has been promoted to the "major league" by starting in the minors.

WHERE SHOULD I BE?

As you work out the logistics of locations, finances, and the positives and negatives of your internship search it should lead you to the ability to answer the last question, where should I be? An internship is a big commitment of time and resources and should be taken very seriously. If you are lucky enough to be required to have an internship by your institution's program you should be fully engaged in finding the right experience for your needs. Resist the urge to use all your efforts on the popular or sexy choices and really go after the experience that will make you the most valuable later. The effort you put in now will pay dividends in the future.

© oatawa/Shutterstock.com

THE FOMO EFFECT

The fear of missing out (FOMO) is a very strong factor and leads to a very stressful situation when a student is asked what they want to do with their life. The pressure of making that choice can paralyze some to inaction. What if the wrong choice is made? What if I miss out on a "better" opportunity? I am so young; how can I possibly know what I want to do with the rest of my life? There are very few choices in life that are permanent, and an internship, or career direction, choice is certainly not one of those. A choice not made, however, is the wrong one. There is a simple test, once you have answered the above questions to the best of your ability, to determine if your choice is correct. Ask yourself the following questions.

- Is it something you think you will enjoy?
- Are you willing to work hard and give your best to the opportunity?

If the answer to those two questions is yes, it is almost impossible to make a wrong choice. You may later determine that you do not enjoy it and want to do something else. Even so, if you have truly given it your best effort it will be noticed and new doors, and careers, will open. It is rare for anyone these days to spend their entire career with one organization. Give your best effort; good things will happen.

CHAPTER 11

Considering When to Apply

K nowing when to apply for an internship can be challenging. First, you must determine your own readiness. You should consider your emotional, academic, and financial readiness but at the same time recognize sometimes opportunities surface that you must pursue, ready or not. But, as a general rule, here are some considerations:

- Do I have the content knowledge and experience (tools) for this particular internship?
- What time of year, semester, or quarter best fits my career goals?
- Will I, or should I, take a full load of classes?
- Will I have extracurricular responsibilities (athletics, campus leadership roles, student organizations, etc.)?
- Is there a pressing family health situation that may limit my availability?
- Is this an opportunity that may not exist for me in the future?

TOOLS

Understanding the position you want and the requirements of that job are critical. If you think of your academic career as a toolbox, then your classes are the tools you need to be successful. Taking business classes like economics, accounting, and finance, or a computer applications class to learn Excel can help you stand out from other candidates. Putting as many tools in the toolbox before applying is important. Most students will be able to complete the job of an intern without much classroom time, but your education allows you to understand why you are doing what you are doing, to understand the organization's reasons for doing it. To get the most out of your experience you need to be as prepared, tool-wise, as you can be. Be honest with yourself as you are going to have to back up what you claim.

© Juris Kraulis/Shutterstock.com

ACADEMICS

The sport, entertainment, and venue management industry is unique in many ways. One way is the seasonality of the different events. The NFL is a fall

© icemanphotos/Shutterstock.com

sport, the NBA and NHL winter, MLB summer. Indoor facilities, arenas, may be less busy in summer but outdoor venues, amphitheaters and even stadiums, are very active with entertainment events. This adds an interesting dynamic to your academic career. There is always something to learn, even in the off season, so no time is a "wrong" time to complete an internship. Still, most students will prefer to complete their internship in-season and this may conflict with a traditional four-year academic degree program. Students should also keep in mind, when they are working on a plan to complete an internship during a regular academic semester or quarter, that academic time off like fall or spring break will not be recognized by your internship employer.

You are in college now and, most likely, of adult age. There are very few career paths that offer three-month summer vacations like a student gets. You should be doing something with this time to make yourself stand out, to be more valuable to employers. Summers, for students in sport, entertainment, and venue management programs, are commonly used for internships but there are other alternatives as well. You can, with proper planning, position yourself to complete a full-time internship in the fall or spring months by taking summer school classes. One benefit of a full-time internship during the semester is that students rarely choose this route, so there is less competition. Students who want to pursue this option should work with their advisors to formulate a plan.

Many freshmen today arrive at college with some sort of college credit from AP courses, dual-enrollment courses, and the like. These extra credits can also be helpful to students who wish to leverage these credits to allow for a longer experience. Imagine being ahead in your academic career by a semester. You could, if the NFL is your thing, take an NFL internship that starts in late June or early July and work for the entire season, returning to school for the spring semester. There are details that would need to be worked out, such as when, which semester, and whether you need to register for an internship or place-holder class, depending on the requirements of your program. Again, working with your academic advisor or faculty mentor will be critical to bring this sort of plan to fruition.

Finally, the internship is often the entry-level position for this industry. Some of these positions may be season or year-long. They may be called an academy or a training program or an internship. An experience of this nature will be something you do after you have completed all classroom-based academic work. Thus, it is important that you identify and understand the seasonality of your chosen direction in the industry early in your academic career. Maybe your choice is baseball and the hiring process starts in early December at the Winter Meetings with final hires made early the next year. You will need to have a plan in place to finish your classes in time to compete for these competitive positions. Many organizations have calendar, or fiscal, year-long internships. Again, early identification is critical for planning purposes.

The sooner you identify organizations, or even specific internships, that you want to work with the better your ability to plan your academic career to meet these goals. Use every possible avenue to make yourself the most valuable hire, in the best time period, you can.

CLASSES

Other experiences (as described in Chapter 5) will be included as part of a regular semester and completed while you are enrolled in classes, but, ideally, full-time internships should be taken when you are not enrolled in any classes, or when you are enrolled in internship-related classes for credit. Every school defines full-time differently and will also have, if available in your program, different regulations concerning what is required for internships to count for class credit. It is critical for a student to understand the expectations for their program and institution, as being a full-time student will have a direct bearing on items like financial aid, student fees, and access to student amenities and services.

Some programs may have limits on whether other classes can be completed during a for-credit internship and may have predetermined courses to add to the internship learning experience. It is important that you have full command of what will be expected from you by your institution or program (minimum

© Matej Kastelic/Shutterstock.com

hours, journals, and other homework) and also by the organization for which you are an intern. It is imperative that both of these situations are congruent with your own situation.

You must also ask yourself whether it is in your best interest to be involved in a class while working, hopefully, a full-time internship. It is unlikely that professors are going to allow you to miss classes for internship responsibilities, so will it work? Are you taking a class load that would make it difficult for you to give the proper attitude and effort to the hiring organization? Would that hurt your reputation? A full-time internship is a large time commitment and the hours will vary a great deal. It is most likely that you will not be able to be as successful as you want, and need, to be in your internship while taking classes as well.

EXTRACURRICULARS

A well-rounded college experience often includes extracurricular activities such as intercollegiate athletics, club sports, Greek life, student organizations, student government, etc. Often these activities will lead to leadership roles. Foresight and planning are needed to keep yourself out of a situation where you need to make a choice between an internship and an active leadership role in student life. An internship is a long-term job interview and asking for time off to be the rush chair is not the best idea. Splitting time, attention, and effort between work and extracurricular activities is also not a good idea no matter how capable you think you are. It is best to focus on your internship when you have committed the time, money, and effort to complete one.

For athletes the decision on when to complete an internship is much more difficult. Other considerations such as in-season or out of season, how long the season runs into the semester of choice for the internship, and other, "volunteer," team-related activities out of season must be considered. Any athlete competing at the collegiate level has a heavy burden on their time, but an internship is no less critical for their success after their playing days are complete. Hopefully your program, or athletic department, has experience handling the realities of a student-athlete completing an internship and can lend some guidance. Every athlete will have to face the end of their playing days at some point and should make that decision for themselves. What is important, however, is that an athlete who wants to work in this industry be honest with themselves in determining when to complete an internship necessary for their post-competition career.

Again, this is a unique industry and many extracurriculars may not be as highly valued as in other industries or as much as real-world work experiences. Use caution when trying to balance the two and ask yourself, "Will what I want to do make me more valuable to a possible employer?"

FAMILY CONSIDERATIONS

Family situations can arise unexpectedly. An unexpected illness or crisis will have to be handled as it occurs. Other times you will know if one of your parents or siblings is especially ill and that your presence will be needed at home more. Perhaps a parent or guardian has lost a job and you now need to ensure that you have a paid internship to help pay bills, thus limiting your options. These issues, while truly out of your control, will definitely impact when you can apply. Working with your advisor or with an internship coordinator may provide some guidance for you.

© Africa Studio/Shutterstock.com

Family issues within your control revolve around events planned well in advance, such as weddings, a sibling's graduation, or a regular family vacation taken at the same time each year. Often these dates are known well in advance so that you can plan accordingly. Remember, as stated numerous times, internships are long job interviews and requesting time off would be frowned upon. Time off for vacations in particular may leave a bad impression with the employer. Ask yourself if you would trade a vacation now for the job in the field you want later. If the answer is no perhaps you are in the wrong field.

OPPORTUNITY

Do you have a unique opportunity that won't be there next year or next semester? Maybe an organization had a late cancellation and needs to fill a spot. Maybe a venue is hosting a large-scale event, such as a major golf tournament that rotates throughout the country, that won't be back. Perhaps your school has partnered with an organization working a world-class event such as the Olympics. In these cases, ready or not, you may have to dive in.

While these, for the most part (except maybe the late-cancellation scenario), will be highly competitive opportunities, you should ask yourself, "Am I prepared?" This may be difficult to ascertain on your own, so rely on professors and mentors to help. Some questions to ask yourself include:

- Have I had work experience, did I receive solid reviews, was it comparable? The experiences you have had previously will have a direct correlation for the hiring entity and also for you.
- Did I enjoy it?
- How many classes in my major have I had and are they appropriate to this experience? Have I learned the needed skills in the job description?
- Do I think I know what I am getting into? Perhaps it is an experience requiring you to work outside on your feet for long periods. Have you had an experience where you spent many hours on your feet? How did you react to it? Do you believe you can do that for multiple days/weeks?
- Am I someone others look to for leadership? Is that something the description mentions? Is this a trait I can portray in my resume?
- Am I self-motivated? This is a question you should ask for just about every experience in this industry.
- Am I really ready for anything? Do I have the ability to adjust to a new reality with minor adjustments?

In the end those hiring will determine your suitability and, if it is an experience you want, you should go after it. It is important in these situations, and really in any situation, not to limit yourself by doubting your abilities. Many times organizations are willing to teach you the skills required if they believe you can provide the necessary attitude and effort. Be realistic to a point, but, if you want it, make the hiring folks tell you that you are not qualified. Say yes and figure it out.

CHAPTER 12

Preparing Application Materials

I t is time to prepare your application materials as part of your internship search. Hopefully you have an advisor, friend, or parent who can help you both brainstorm what to include in your materials, and also how to best organize your information. Your institution likely has a career office or other entity offering advice on resumes and cover letters. You are encouraged to schedule an appointment with the appropriate person in a timely fashion. Your program's faculty may also be able to add input. Different persons will offer you varying advice and you have to find how to best incorporate tidbits from each individual while staying true to yourself. If you have access to industry professionals, getting their feedback would be invaluable.

Many employers ask that application materials be submitted electronically, either through their own in-house system or via a third party. There are many free third-party sites, such as teamworkonline.com, with whom it would be beneficial for you to establish an account. Some of these companies offer free trials for extended services, allowing you to make your own choice on how to best allocate your finances devoted to the job search.

RESUME

What jobs, volunteer opportunities, and/or internships have you held/completed in the sport, entertainment, and venue industries? What jobs or philanthropic endeavors have you worked and what leadership positions have you held in these areas? What awards have you won? You should write down everything that fits in one of these three lists. Eventually you will have to make decisions since at this stage in your career most professionals would suggest a one-page resume. High school accomplishments should be the first casualty.

Avoid identifying membership in political organizations unless it directly relates to a position because there is no reason to irk 50% of the hiring committee before the process starts, regardless of your affiliation. Some companies hold strong negative stereotypes concerning Greek organizations and you should also use caution identifying your letters unless it relates to the position or unless someone has told you definitively that the hiring manager was also a member. Leadership in church or religious organizations is usually acceptable but simply identifying your place of worship would not be necessary.

It is a good practice to keep one "master" resume with all of your experiences and accomplishments included and then create an application-specific "one-pager" as you apply for different positions. As you describe your experiences keep in mind that you are trying to match your skills and abilities with the employer's needs. Your "one-pager" should include tangible, transferable skills that you have. These may include:

© hvostik/Shutterstock.com

- Ability to work in a team setting
- Proven leadership skills
- Communication
- Work ethic

- Analytical and technical skills
- Organized and detail oriented
- Ability to be flexible and adaptable
- Initiative

As you work to describe your experiences be sure to use appropriate action verbs. A quick internet search will give you plenty of material for relating experiences and allow you to really make your resume stand out in areas the job description identifies. Make your resume stand out and tell those hiring that you are a person they need to interview.

One last note on your resume, be completely honest with your employer and with yourself. Be sure you can actually deliver on the skills you say you hold.

COVER LETTER

The cover letter arguably is more important than the resume. It is the document a hiring manager reads first and will lead him or her to reviewing your resume with great interest or immediately discarding it. It is important to recognize that your cover letters need to be individualized. Always address the individual by name and title. This may require a little research as well. A call to the organization's HR department may get you the needed information. You can't apply for 20 internships with the same letter except for changing the organization's name. Also, this is a small industry and hiring professionals speak to each other. You can never be sure who knows who and the use of a "form" letter may be damaging to your chances. Sending this "form" letter with incorrect information will all but end your candidacy.

Each organization has a different mission and focus, and your job is to demonstrate how your interests and experiences fit the agency to the point that they want to consider you. The cover letter is also your opportunity to show you have researched the organization and understand their mission and focus.

The opening paragraph needs to do this in a dynamic way that is true to your personality. The body should make references to your resume but also must elaborate on specific experiences. Specifics are important:

- Liaised with local Boy Scout and Girl Scout groups and the front office on a Scout night with a minor league hockey franchise (name

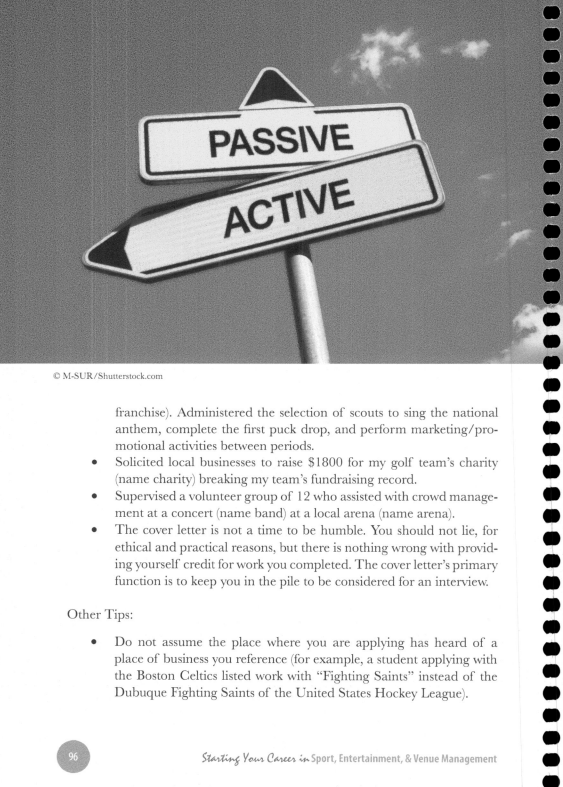

franchise). Administered the selection of scouts to sing the national anthem, complete the first puck drop, and perform marketing/promotional activities between periods.

- Solicited local businesses to raise $1800 for my golf team's charity (name charity) breaking my team's fundraising record.
- Supervised a volunteer group of 12 who assisted with crowd management at a concert (name band) at a local arena (name arena).
- The cover letter is not a time to be humble. You should not lie, for ethical and practical reasons, but there is nothing wrong with providing yourself credit for work you completed. The cover letter's primary function is to keep you in the pile to be considered for an interview.

Other Tips:

- Do not assume the place where you are applying has heard of a place of business you reference (for example, a student applying with the Boston Celtics listed work with "Fighting Saints" instead of the Dubuque Fighting Saints of the United States Hockey League).

If you done it,
it ain't
bragging.

Walt Whitman

© Oleg Golovnev/Shutterstock.com

- Do not use acronyms unless they are common organizations on a national level (NCAA, NFL, FIFA) and be prepared to identify a city and a league of an organization.
- Make sure your contact information is available on the cover letter and the resume. The phone number where you plan to receive calls should not include an inappropriate voicemail message.
- Proofread! Proofread! Proofread! And let someone else proofread it as well. One spelling error could doom you. Hiring managers reinforce what your professors are telling you, that one mistake eliminates you from consideration and your information goes right into the delete folder or the wastebasket.
- Lastly, always say thank you.

PORTFOLIO

Many a career in sport, entertainment, and/or venue management will be a creative one. One way for you to showcase your abilities, to prove you can do what you say, is to create a portfolio. Doing this gives you the opportunity to showcase skills that may be of value to employers. Perhaps it is using an application such as Photoshop or other creative software. Maybe it is showcasing your writing skills on stories, bios, or press releases. Creating a portfolio gives you another chance to stand out.

© art4all/Shutterstock.com

> "There is not just one (characteristic). At every step along the way, we have looked for people that are authentic, willing to grind, care about people, know what they are doing, have a results-oriented mindset, and do it all with great integrity."
>
> *Danny Morrison • President • Carolina Panthers (2009-2017)*

> "Event people are in the experience business with a major emphasis on customer service. Great attitude is a 100% priority and needs to be 'habitual' not just something that gets switched on when one thinks of it."
>
> *Craig Lovett • Partner/Principal • Incognitus*

CHAPTER 13

Your Social Media Presence

Today's college-age students seeking internships have grown up in an era where the use of social media is automatic. There is a myriad of applications that allow persons to express themselves and share important moments in their lives. Social media include websites and applications that enable users to create and share content or to participate in social networking.

It is important for internship seekers to have the right social media presence. Most students have undoubtedly been warned by someone that prospective employers and other important persons are reviewing their social media

accounts. The legality of the use of such employer-found information varies but companies are reviewing applicant profiles in search of red flags or fit. This can include proclivity to inappropriate or unprofessional behavior or holding extreme political views contrary to the organization's mission. It can include not only what someone posts directly but what someone likes or shares.

The use of derogatory, vulgar, or offensive terms should be obvious. But other posts may be employer-dependent. Some agencies will not care about a picture of a family gathering where the applicant is holding a bottle of beer but others will be concerned. A student applying for an internship at a sporting goods store may have no reason to worry about an account of their hunting or target shooting efforts but must recognize that other entities may find gun possession contrary to their values. The sport industry conducts business with members of all political parties, so students should be careful not to explicitly identify their political affiliations in social media posts.

So how can students use social media effectively, especially during the internship search and beyond? They should have a clean profile and build a professional presence online.

CLEAN PROFILE

This chapter has already identified that prospective employers do review social media sites and that some will go to great lengths to find out about the social media personas of potential hirees. Students should feel free to post their accomplishments at school, their work, and on their teams. Consistency on all social media sites in this area is important. They can certainly also like and share stories from their favorite teams when they win a big game, provided the team is not a rival to a place the student plans on applying. Pictures of special moments with family or friends are also appropriate. Check back over your profiles, as it would be a shame to have a post from three years ago take you out of the running for a position. These positions are highly competitive and sometimes it is little things like a social media profile that are the difference.

LinkedIn should definitely be a place where a prospective applicant has a presence. Students should work with their institutional mentors to build the best profile. It is known that a large percentage of recruiters are searching using this medium. Companies also use LinkedIn to post information about their company.

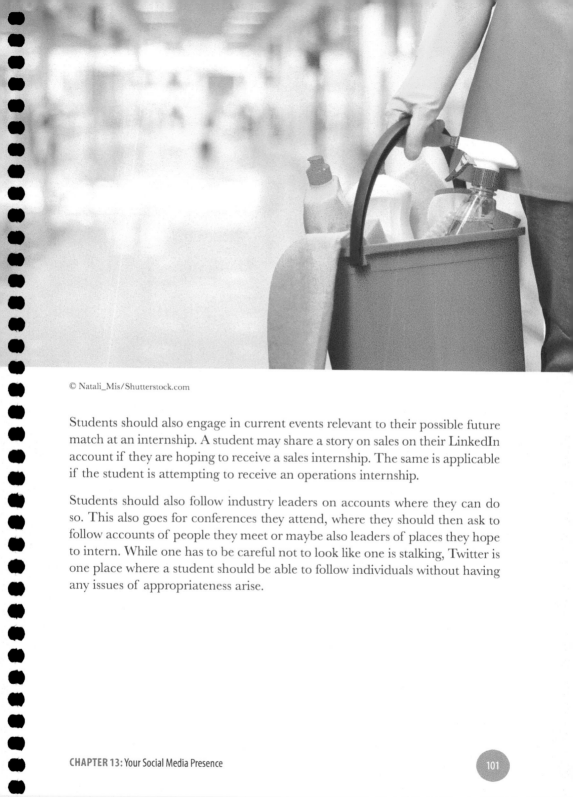

© Natali_Mis/Shutterstock.com

Students should also engage in current events relevant to their possible future match at an internship. A student may share a story on sales on their LinkedIn account if they are hoping to receive a sales internship. The same is applicable if the student is attempting to receive an operations internship.

Students should also follow industry leaders on accounts where they can do so. This also goes for conferences they attend, where they should then ask to follow accounts of people they meet or maybe also leaders of places they hope to intern. While one has to be careful not to look like one is stalking, Twitter is one place where a student should be able to follow individuals without having any issues of appropriateness arise.

CHAPTER 14

Receiving and Negotiating the Offer

Congratulations, you have received an offer to complete an internship! The offer may have come from a first choice or even an only choice, at which point acceptance may appear to be a fairly easy decision. You need to know what your next steps are. You may have received this offer while still holding out and awaiting word from other places for which you have applied. You are unsure how to best navigate this. Hopefully this chapter will offer you some insights on both of these situations.

RECEIVED THE FIRST CHOICE

You are undoubtedly excited to receive the offer you wanted. However, you should still use due diligence before making the final decision. You should get the offer in writing. This may or may not include signatures needed by your institution. You need to determine whether you get paid at all, a monthly

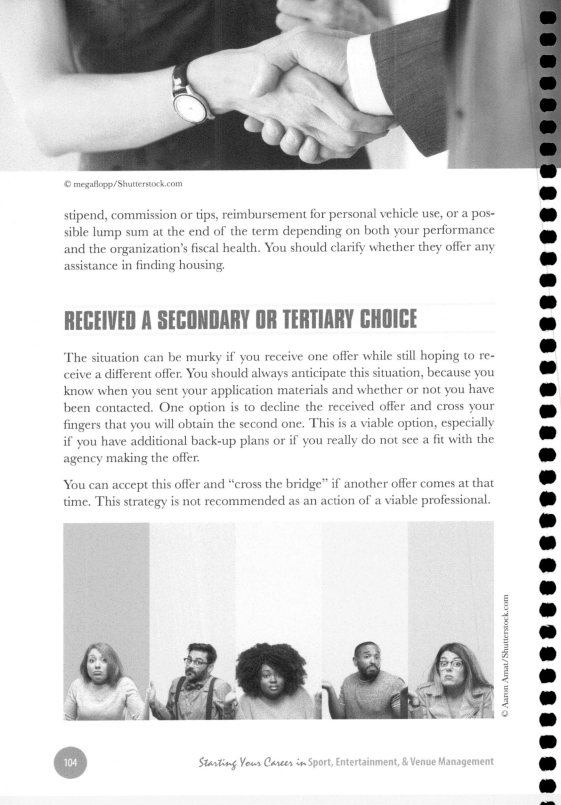

stipend, commission or tips, reimbursement for personal vehicle use, or a possible lump sum at the end of the term depending on both your performance and the organization's fiscal health. You should clarify whether they offer any assistance in finding housing.

RECEIVED A SECONDARY OR TERTIARY CHOICE

The situation can be murky if you receive one offer while still hoping to receive a different offer. You should always anticipate this situation, because you know when you sent your application materials and whether or not you have been contacted. One option is to decline the received offer and cross your fingers that you will obtain the second one. This is a viable option, especially if you have additional back-up plans or if you really do not see a fit with the agency making the offer.

You can accept this offer and "cross the bridge" if another offer comes at that time. This strategy is not recommended as an action of a viable professional.

You can also ask for an extension. You would need to be honest when making the ask, recognize it risks alienating the company, and realize such a request may be denied. Veteran hiring managers understand there is competition for good people and likely have seen this situation many times before and will appreciate the honesty. Some, however, may not view this positively and will move on to another candidate.

It is unusual that an extension would be for more than a week and 48 hours is more likely if one is granted. Where you as a candidate are in the overall depth chart of other applicants will likely be a major determinant and you will not know where you stand. Should you receive an extension, you then need to contact the place you hope to intern and explain the situation. Your hope is they can expedite the process or let you know that you are not a serious candidate. The depth of the applicant pool for this other site will also likely dictate their response.

If the extension lapses or is not offered, you have a decision to make. The ethical dilemma occurs when you accept the first offer but later receive the one you wanted. You may have the following thoughts:

- Aren't contracts always broken anyway?
- Won't they be fine without me?
- Someone else will receive the opportunity, right?
- Should I really turn down the opportunity of a lifetime to help propel MY career?

An ethical decision maker and reflective thinker must be careful not to rationalize for personal gain. While some contracts are broken, they are not always broken. If they were, there would be no need for them because they would not mean anything.

Yes, the organization will be fine without you and likely another person will receive your opportunity, but that cannot be an ethical consideration. The fourth question bears thought.

You should have these thoughts as well:

- How much damage will I do to my reputation?
- Is it possible this will harm me with other organizations? Does the first offer organization have a relationship with anyone at my preferred choice?

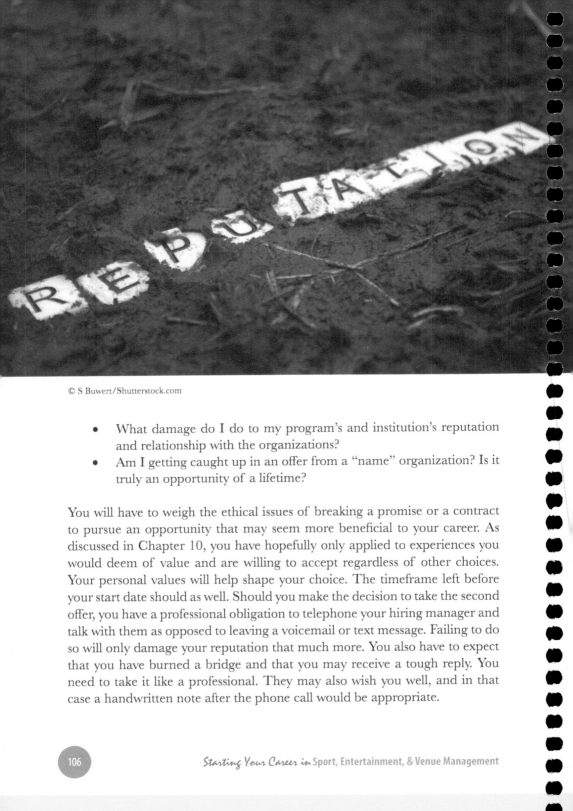

- What damage do I do to my program's and institution's reputation and relationship with the organizations?
- Am I getting caught up in an offer from a "name" organization? Is it truly an opportunity of a lifetime?

You will have to weigh the ethical issues of breaking a promise or a contract to pursue an opportunity that may seem more beneficial to your career. As discussed in Chapter 10, you have hopefully only applied to experiences you would deem of value and are willing to accept regardless of other choices. Your personal values will help shape your choice. The timeframe left before your start date should as well. Should you make the decision to take the second offer, you have a professional obligation to telephone your hiring manager and talk with them as opposed to leaving a voicemail or text message. Failing to do so will only damage your reputation that much more. You also have to expect that you have burned a bridge and that you may receive a tough reply. You need to take it like a professional. They may also wish you well, and in that case a handwritten note after the phone call would be appropriate.

NEGOTIATION

When you have to decided to accept the offer for the organization you want, there may be room for negotiation. Money is probably not an area where there will be much movement as companies have to save their negotiation for full-time employees. You can ask about housing arrangements, as previously indicated, and this is the opportunity to request time off for the special family occasion. Examples would be a sibling's marriage and would not include a three-day vacation with friends. This can be a very difficult ask and should be avoided—barring the previously mentioned family wedding. One thing to keep in mind as you work through this is that this experience is your chance to make a great impression and, potentially, earn a full-time position. Asking for time off may not be the best thing to do when looking at it like that.

You may also need to negotiate start date or finish date. Your college may not end their preceding semester in a manner that accommodates the site's schedule and there will be little you can do about it. Are you available during some weekends during the preceding semester where you can work, even if you have to drive a few hours? Are there some projects you can start on remotely, recognizing your institution may not allow you to count the hours? Being willing to do extra is never a bad thing.

You may be a student-athlete who has to report early for training camp. You should have disclosed this before the offer was made but now would be the time to finalize this. You have to recognize they may not allow you to miss as much time as you would like and so you need to be in communication with your coach. Maybe they want you to stay after your school's next semester starts because of a big event. If the event promises to be a great experience, you may have need to ask your school if you can start late or save the resources to make a return trip to your destination.

CONCLUSION

The accepting of an internship is a special time and is a reward for your hard work. However, the process does not automatically end, so do be sure to take these things into consideration when you negotiate to ensure as productive an experience as possible.

"One of the most important attributes we look for is a positive attitude and being a go-getter. There will be long, hard days where you're exhausted or frustrated but attitude is everything. It gets you through your day faster, others look forward to working with you, and supervisors recognize it and appreciate it."

Holly Skrenes •Senior Director, EM&S Training and Sales Operations • Feld Entertainment

"Attitude will determine your success (or failure) in the event industry. You must be able to accept constant change, demanding promoters and clients, political influences, staffing challenges, and uncontrollable external circumstances. A smile, a laugh, a positive acknowledgement, and always a backup plan are needed to succeed in this industry!"

Cheryl Swanson, CVE • Vice President/General Manager • Columbia Metropolitan Convention Center

SECTION 4

After the Hire

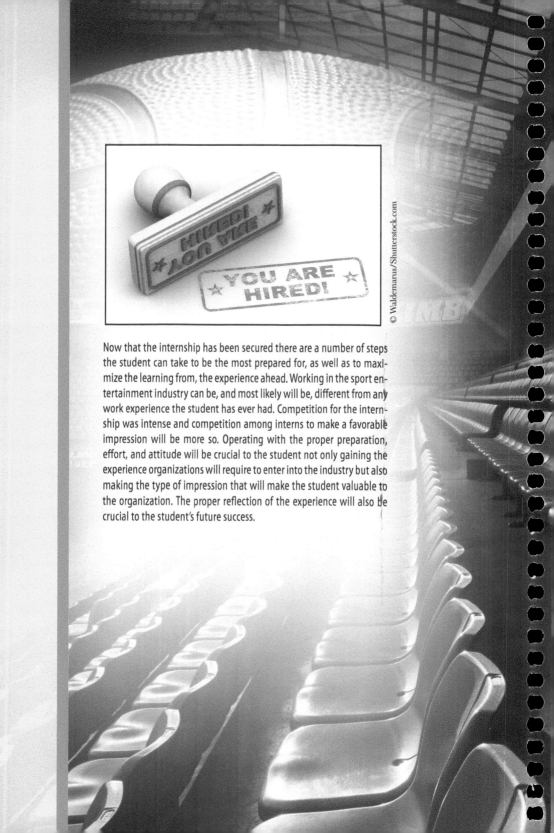

Now that the internship has been secured there are a number of steps the student can take to be the most prepared for, as well as to maximize the learning from, the experience ahead. Working in the sport entertainment industry can be, and most likely will be, different from any work experience the student has ever had. Competition for the internship was intense and competition among interns to make a favorable impression will be more so. Operating with the proper preparation, effort, and attitude will be crucial to the student not only gaining the experience organizations will require to enter into the industry but also making the type of impression that will make the student valuable to the organization. The proper reflection of the experience will also be crucial to the student's future success.

CHAPTER 15

Preparing for the Internship

Again, having the proper preparation, effort, and attitude will be crucial for the student. First, it is imperative that the student learn all they can about the organization with which they will be working. What is the organization's primary business? What is the organization's mission? How do they accomplish that mission? What is the organizational structure? Who are the key executives and managers and what is their background? What can you learn about them before you start?

Example: Imagine a student working in minor league baseball working in the box office. During the internship the student comments to his boss, the box office manager, that the general manager of the team does a terrible job selecting players for the team. The student continues with the assumption that if the team had better players they would win more games. The student states that winning more games would drive up sales and attendance, thus making the team more financially successful as well as being more successful on the field.

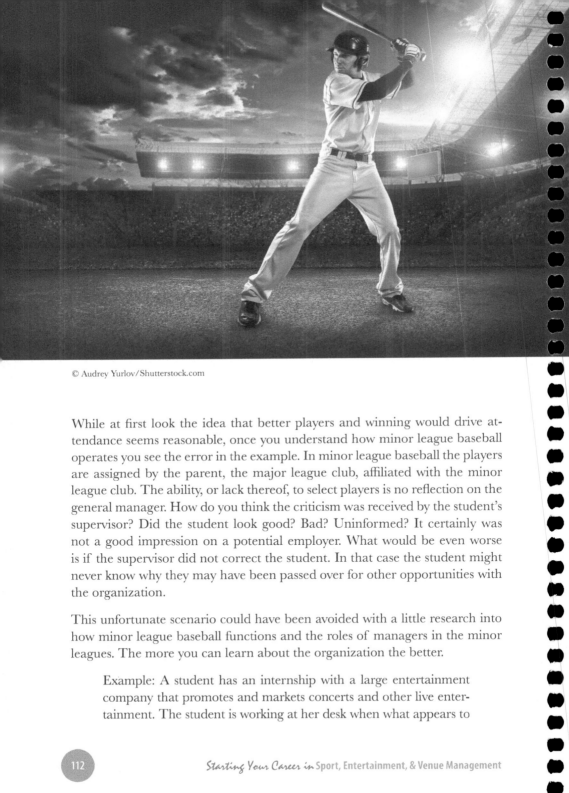

© Audrey Yurlov/Shutterstock.com

While at first look the idea that better players and winning would drive attendance seems reasonable, once you understand how minor league baseball operates you see the error in the example. In minor league baseball the players are assigned by the parent, the major league club, affiliated with the minor league club. The ability, or lack thereof, to select players is no reflection on the general manager. How do you think the criticism was received by the student's supervisor? Did the student look good? Bad? Uninformed? It certainly was not a good impression on a potential employer. What would be even worse is if the supervisor did not correct the student. In that case the student might never know why they may have been passed over for other opportunities with the organization.

This unfortunate scenario could have been avoided with a little research into how minor league baseball functions and the roles of managers in the minor leagues. The more you can learn about the organization the better.

Example: A student has an internship with a large entertainment company that promotes and markets concerts and other live entertainment. The student is working at her desk when what appears to

© Mooshny/Shutterstock.com

be an important company executive walks by and says good morning. The student responds to the greeting in kind but uses the executive's name. Impressed, the executive stops and asks if he knows the student. She responds that she has researched who everyone is. This makes a great impression on the executive and he spends the next 30 minutes with the student discussing who she is, her academic program, and her goals for her internship and career. The executive offers to connect via LinkedIn and for the student to reach out to him whenever she has questions or is in need of advice.

Who would not want to have as a mentor a high-ranking executive in the career field they have chosen? Because this student researched the company she would be working for, including who the main executives and managers are, she was able to make a connection that will have a long-term impact on her career.

You should be prepared to present yourself appropriately. In the sport, entertainment, and venue world appropriate dress can vary wildly from business formal to cut-off shorts and t-shirts. You will have an idea about the appropriate attire from your interview but it does not hurt to ask as well. Once you have a good idea what to wear it is a very good idea to overdress your first day. You do not have to spend a lot of money on clothing, just be sure you are attired appropriately. Personal grooming will also be important. There will be time later to be a "free spirit" but, for now, it is important to keep in mind who you are working for and what their expectations will be. That first impression can never be undone, and you want to make it the best you can.

Another important aspect of your attire is your footwear. You may spend many hours on your feet and protecting them can save a great deal of pain. An investment in a good pair of shoes will go a long way to making sure you can stay on your feet and make a great impression on your supervisor.

Lastly, to be fully prepared, an extra change of clothes, including shoes, is a must. There are times on the job when manual labor needs to be completed, especially if you are working for a smaller organization where every employee wears a number of hats. Having a second set of "work" clothes for the dirty jobs is a good idea. If you are not in a position to have that sort of job, there are still reasons to carry a change of clothes. For example, you may be working outside and get caught in bad weather. Sometimes things come up and you need to be prepared.

This type of preparation can set you apart from other interns, and, while many will hear this advice, few will actually go to these lengths to be this pre-pared. Taking the extra steps, going above and beyond, will set you apart and help you reach the goals you desire.

CHAPTER 16

Opening Day

You have done almost all of your preparation and are almost ready for the first day of work. You must never, especially the opening day, be late for work. Your last bit of preparation is to make a practice run to your location a day or two in advance of your start. It is worthwhile to make this practice run to your place of employment at exactly the time you need to be there so you can understand traffic patterns, trains, account for time to find parking, get from your mode of transportation to the office, etc. Again, do not be late. This sort of mistake is almost inexcusable.

Now you are ready. You must present the proper attitude and effort needed to be successful in making the kind of impression you desire to create. It is very important to remember that the job you have as an intern will, most likely, not be the job you aspire to after graduation or in the near term once you have begun your career. Interns tend to be the lowest ranking employee in the organization. As such they, the interns, will receive assignments, "intern jobs," which are less desirable than they may wish. It may be stuffing envelopes and

© Stokkete/Shutterstock.com

answering phones or it could be your turn to clean the concourse bathrooms. Your attitude and effort in handling these assignments will be critical. If you are lucky enough to be in a highly competitive internship, like with an NFL or MLB team, with a large concert promotion organization, or with a major arena, there are hundreds, and maybe more, students who wish they were in your place and keeping that in mind will help you keep your attitude and effort where they should be.

Your attitude toward your internship should be one of gratitude for the opportunity and a desire to do and learn all you can. In this industry there are potential negatives in the hours you will work. They are numerous and often happen at times, nights, weekends, and holidays, when friends and family are enjoying themselves. Working in the sport, entertainment, and/or venue management industry means you work when others have fun. If you work for the Detroit Lions you are always working Thanksgiving Day. Perhaps you are with the past year's NBA champion; your Christmas day is almost guaranteed to be a work day. How many music festivals occur during the Fourth of July? As an intern completing an internship in a spring semester the likelihood of you getting time off for spring break is very low. The job of an industry manager is

to provide moments to others. You will very likely not receive much in the way of monetary compensation while you are working. This also can work against a student and their ability to maintain a positive attitude toward the work. A negative attitude can and will show through quickly and have a dire effect on the student's quality of work. If you understand and accept these realities before your first day on the job it will be much easier to keep working with a smile on your face and a great attitude.

Your effort will also be critical to your success. The ability to continue to give great effort while those around you want to quit will help you stand out. You will be asked to do some tasks you will not be thrilled to do. You must complete every task to the best of your abilities, and not just the large ones but the small ones as well. Attention to the smallest tasks often makes the largest tasks easy. Again, this is a great opportunity and employers are looking for people who are willing to do what is necessary to be successful.

Attitude and effort can show through in a number of ways:

> Scenario 1: There are two students working similar operations jobs in two NFL stadiums. The first student works in a place where they use a pickup truck to move items around the stadium. It can be driven all over the stadium. The operations crew typically use it as

a meeting room table, lunch room, and garbage can. On a particular day, as the crew was breaking up a lunch meeting, the manager asked the student to clean the truck out. The student said cleaning the truck was not what he signed up for and refused to clean out the truck. The second student, also in operations, spent most of his internship volunteering for every job that came available. It might have been painting bathrooms or cleaning storerooms. It did not matter; if it needed being done, he wanted to do it. He showed up early and left late, making sure every task was complete.

What should the supervisor do with the first student? Did the student behave appropriately? What is the appropriate response? In this scenario the student was terminated from his internship for refusing to clean the truck (and some other attitude issues). While few would be as brazen as to outright refuse the assignment, many interns would approach the task half-heartedly, potentially reducing their effectiveness and taking longer to complete the task, and, perhaps, complain about the assignment to others, displaying their poor attitude. This can lead to supervisors having little faith in the intern's ability to handle larger, more important, roles. As an intern you may have to do jobs that are unappealing. The best way to handle them is to just jump in and get them done. An important thing to keep in mind is that once you begin your career as a manager you may have interns working for you. You will certainly have temporary and part-time employees. Being an intern gives you the insight needed to understand what these employees are going through on the job and, hopefully, make you a better manager.

© Jurgis Mankauskas/Shutterstock.com

The second intern in this scenario was often harassed by other interns as someone who was trying to curry favor with the supervisors by volunteering for everything. This did not stop him from grasping the opportunity at hand by looking for extra tasks to complete. In your internship you should try to not sit idle. Ask for work. If your supervisor has none, ask if you can see if anyone else has anything you can help with. At the end of his internship the supervisor asked him about this and about why he volunteered for everything the way he did. The student replied that when he left that final day his supervisor would remember him, and miss him, and that he wanted a job with that stadium. The supervisor did miss him and he did offer him a job at the end of his academic career. Take full advantage of your internship and do as much as you can to stand out.

> Scenario 2: A student is working for a minor league baseball team and his supervisor is the stadium operations manager. The student is complaining to his professor that his internship supervisor is being too hard on him. The student explains that every day when the supervisor comes in he, the student, is the only intern told to complete the daily opening tasks for the stadium. The student explains that there are five other interns in the department, but he is the only one told to complete the tasks. The student believes this is unfair as he is the only person being asked to complete the tasks while the other interns complete menial tasks or sit idle waiting for the gates to open.

Does this student have the correct attitude in regards to this situation? What can be inferred from the supervisor's behavior? How should this situation be handled by the student? One thing that was clear to the professor was that the student had made a mistake. The professor believed that he could infer that the supervisor only assigned these tasks to the one student because that student was the only one the supervisor could trust to complete the tasks in the manner required. The professor further explained that this student's mistake was to miss an incredible opportunity to take ownership of the tasks and complete them without being instructed. The student knew what needed to be done each day and could have made an even more favorable impression by just doing the tasks. He could have shown leadership skills by taking one of the other interns to assist.

> Scenario 3: A student worked for an agency in New York. The agency represents athletes and performers in contract negotiations and in marketing themselves. She worked with and for a senior agent with many top clients. Over the course of her internship she picked up

many new tasks and completed them to the best of her ability and in a timely manner. She was always pleasant and always willing to do whatever needed to be done (notes from her supervisor on her evaluation form). At the end of her internship her supervisor offered her a full-time position instead of going back to school. She turned it down to complete her education. Her supervisor countered by offering her the position when she graduated. She informed him it would be 18 months and he accepted and told her the job would be waiting.

This opportunity, in the form of an internship, regardless of how long it runs, is an opportunity to make a great impression on an organization that will need entry-level employees soon. Every organization has turnover because the industry is so demanding of what would normally be leisure time (nights, weekends, and holidays) and because of low starting pay. If you treat your internship as a job interview in which you want to present the best image of yourself that you can, you will be much better served. Organizations can and will make room for students who have impressed them. Not every task you complete in an internship will be glamorous or fun but no task should be beneath you. All tasks should be attempted with great effort and a great attitude. If you use that approach you just may leave your internship with the entry-level job you desire.

© Rawpixel.com/Shutterstock.com

> "Every employee should appreciate the unique opportunity we have to work in the events/venue business. We bring the fun to everyone! Learn from your mentors, seek guidance from the other departments, and capitalize on every teachable moment. We may not control our destinies, but we can learn a lot along the way!"
>
> *Cheryl Swanson, CVE • Vice President/General Manager • Columbia Metropolitan Convention Center*

> "Work takes up 65% of our lives. Get into a space that you are happy at work in. Get around motivating people and into a crew/team that truly cares about the welfare of each other and demonstrate an attitude of respect at all times."
>
> *Craig Lovett • Partner/Principal • Incognitus*

CHAPTER 17

Mentors

Students will be exposed to different mentors at their organization site, with the site's relevant partners, and with the faculty and staff at their host institution. These contacts have the potential of becoming lasting relationships as part of a student's professional network. The mentors will be able to help the students adjust to new surroundings and learn from different situations and professionals. How best should you seek mentorship and grow from their experiences?

INSTITUTION

Each institution has its own procedures concerning the supervision of student interns, both for credit-seeking and non-credit-seeking students. This could range from senior tenured faculty serving as the primary mentor as part of their overall teaching load, a junior or non-titled faculty member whose primary responsibility is internship supervision, or a staff member representing a college's centralized academic internship office.

Students should place value on this relationship regardless of who their institutional supervisor is. You may not have had a course with this individual or have any previous relationship with them, but you should take the initiative to schedule a meeting with this individual to introduce yourself and share with them your goals for your experience. Having knowledge of the supervisor's background and professional network is important as well and can be of assistance to your ability to grow from working with them.

Students should also seek out professors who teach in a specialty that they have interest in. It may be a professor or instructor who teaches a higher level of a specific subject such as marketing, sales, or analytics. These professors have experiences, be they theoretical research or practical applications, to assist the student in understanding the specifics of the tasks they may face in an internship. This will be critical as you are applying what you have learned in the field.

The role of your institutional mentor will vary depending on your institution, but you should be able to trust them in their ability to assist you in important roles.

INTERNSHIP SITE

You will also have both official and unofficial mentors at your host organization. The official mentor will be someone assigned as your immediate supervisor. Depending on your organization, this may be a person who oversees all interns or it may be someone specific to your primary area of concentration.

Your unofficial mentors include anyone you build a rapport with, who is easy to talk to, and who is comfortable offering advice. They may or may not be younger professionals like you, and they may or may not be in your immediate area, but they will be invaluable in your growth in the industry.

Regardless of how you connect with these mentors it is important to build relationships with them. You do this through conversation, asking questions about the job, but also about your career path. Many will be happy to assist a young professional who shows a real desire to learn and an appreciation of the opportunity.

OTHER MENTOR OPPORTUNITIES

These mentors may come from the research you completed on the industry in Chapter 7. They may come from smaller experiences you have completed like short-term or long-term volunteering. Again, communication is critical. Relationships like mentor/mentee do not happen without communication and you expressing a desire to be mentored.

SCENARIOS

The following examples shed some light on situations and how your different mentors can be of assistance to your learning.

Scenario #1

You witnessed a senior co-worker go off script and blatantly lie to a prospective client in an attempt to make a sale. This co-worker is not part of your own chain of command. You may be conflicted on whether to report this to their supervisor, confront the co-worker directly, or ignore it. A mentor can offer objective advice.

Scenario #2

You are interning with an organization where the majority of interns and junior staff members party frequently while off work. You are not comfortable at such gatherings where persons are becoming intoxicated and thus rarely go out with the group. However, you now feel left out of inside jokes and subsequent professional opportunities. A mentor can help you navigate this situation.

Scenario #3

You perceive a fellow intern is flirting with you. You do not have any romantic feelings for this person and do not believe you have given any signals to the contrary. The fellow intern is not saying inappropriate things, touching you, or anything else that would meet any definition of sexual harassment. However, you are uncomfortable around this person and are equally tentative about letting them know. A mentor may be able to offer you the best advice.

Scenario #4

A student is working on a marketing campaign for a sports team. The marketing directors are going with a strategy that features the best promotions on the games already most likely to sell well. The students remembers in class differing opinions on this marketing strategy. They are excited to share what they learned in that meeting and how it relates to their previous class sessions.

Scenario #5

You are not being used in the way the job description advertised and your shifts have become de facto gym supervisions with no other duties at any time. This has been a regular and not an isolated occurrence. A mentor from your institution may need to get involved as this may contradict the regulations guiding internships.

In each of the scenarios the student has a mentor at their institution, ideally familiar with them and also with the institution's policies and ethics, with whom to discuss things. Conversations would stay private except in circumstances outlined to students where the law or institutional policies prohibit such privacy.

SUMMARY

Your mentors will come from different areas and will have several responsibilities toward you. You also will have a responsibility to lean on the mentor as necessary and maximize the learning from those relationships. These mentors will go beyond just your internships as well. If you have developed the relationships, mentors can last a lifetime. As you move forward in your career it is important to remember those who have come before you and helped you and return the favor to those who will come after.

CHAPTER 18

Learning on the Job

Very few will have the position they long for in their internship. You may be working for an organization that you truly wish to work for but the duties and responsibilities will not be a "dream" position. There will, however, still be a great deal to be learned and much of this can be accomplished through asking the right questions of those doing the job and reflection. Keeping a record of the who, what, where, when, how, and, most importantly, why of your internship can be critical to your learning success.

JOURNALS

Journaling is a great way to keep a record of what you have done and what you have learned and should be done in a specific way. Your internship will hopefully be of a significant length, 12 to 15 weeks. Completing a journal entry every two weeks will provide you with a great learning opportunity and provide you with a record for later reflection as well. The journal should be a record of your activities undertaken during each two-week period. It should include the tasks and projects you completed and any that you may have seen but were not a direct participant in. These records should include who you worked with, what you did, where the tasks were accomplished, and how you accomplished them. The same criteria can be used for projects only seen and not worked on. As an example of one journal entry:

> This week I worked on a school reading project with our marketing coordinator and director of community relations. We visited an elementary school to read to a couple of kindergarten classes. I was dressed up in the mascot uniform and was able to read to the kids. The mascot uniform is disgusting and incredibly hard to see out of but it was a lot of fun to interact with the students and they really appreciated us being there.

A section like the example above should be completed for every task you undertake, regardless how inconsequential you may think it is. Very few organizations create what you might call busy work for the intern to complete. Organizations hire interns for multiple reasons, including giving back and talent identification. They have a purpose in mind and, to the organization, everything you do has some importance attached to it.

This leads us to the last, and most important, part of the journal. It is also where most of the intern's learning will take place: the why. The why should

© Sorn340 Images/Shutterstock.com

include why the task is necessary to complete. Why is it important to the organization? How does it fit into the overall mission of the organization? The intern may have a good idea of the answer to these questions but, as is the case with most questions in the industry, it will depend on the circumstances for that organization. To get to the answers specific to the organization they are interning with they should ask. Going back to the above example:

> How does the program work? Is this program strictly to build good PR in the community? Is it an attempt to build an affinity for our club amongst the students? Do we offer tickets for the students to get their parents to bring them to the game? Sometimes it may be as simple as asking why do we, the organization, do this?

Every organization will have their own reasons for the projects they complete. Knowing the specific whys for each task will allow the student to develop a manager's mentality and allow the student to begin to develop their own management style as well as a better understanding of how managers in their chosen field operate. This may be the most critical piece of the student's education, understanding the why.

Journaling tip: The student should carry a small notepad with them at all times. While most students will have a phone, and technology is great, paper has one distinct advantage over a phone. The batteries in a notepad have never died. By taking notes you cannot forget what you learned. If you are given an assignment, write it down. If something of interest happens, write it down. When you get the answer to one of your why questions, write it down. These notes can be used when you create your journal entries. Do not trust your memory; write it down.

REFLECTION QUESTIONS

To help guide the student's reflection in several critical areas the following questions should be answered. They are designed to help the student assess aspects of the internship they may not think of on their own. While they can be answered in any order that the student, or internship program, may desire, they are laid out in this text as a series of questions answered every two weeks. The answer to these questions will require some thought and some introspection from the student. The answers should not be hurried, and each question can be answered more than once.

Journal 1:

- How many individuals do you work with at your internship site? How many other interns are employed by the site? What are your early impressions on how you will compare?
- What do you perceive as the advantages and disadvantages with the number of employees and fellow interns at your internship site? How might this impact their ability to recruit and retain a talented and diverse workforce?
- Where is your internship located within your community or metropolitan area? How does your site use this location to their advantage? What are the challenges and what strategies are employed to combat them?
- How have you already experienced formal and/or informal mentoring from official supervisors and other employees or business partners?

Journal 2:

- How have you experienced diversity (age, gender, race, religion, sexual orientation, political persuasion, etc.) in your interactions with co-workers, mentors, and clients? How different is it at your site compared to your college and your hometown?
- What have you experienced with respect to the written or unwritten rules regarding protocol, hierarchy, and/or communication at your internship site?
- How would you describe the organizational culture at your site, and how does this fit your style and your "ideal" employer and work-life balance?
- How formally do different people at your site or involved with your site (i.e., clients/customers, etc.) dress? Does this impact personal interactions?

Journal 3:

- How structured is your time during an average day? How much mentoring do you receive on your projects or assignments? Are you comfortable with this current set-up and do you believe it maximizes your contribution to the company?
- How do the events either supported or put on directly by your internship site relate to the purpose and mission statement of the organization?

- Does the organization appear to be an active member of the greater community (however this is defined)? How can the site improve in this area?

Journal 4:

- How does the organization distribute the level of work among the interns? Have you received a sense of how favorably your supervisors think of you in comparison to other interns or co-workers? Are you receiving more challenging assignments than your co-workers or is the scenario flipped?
- What types of tasks are you discovering that you enjoy or excel at completing? Which ones are less attractive or fulfilling?
- Describe the way in which the organization collaborates with competitors in the industry.

Journal 5:

- How does the internship site incorporate their organizational mission into their daily operations?
- How have you networked effectively both on and off the clock? How have you built both your professional network and your personal brand? What opportunities have you missed and what would you do differently if you were provided a second chance?
- What do you need to do to follow in the career path of one of your current co-workers or mentors?

Journal 6:

- What experiences have you endured with colleagues, or with how your site handled something, that left a bad taste in your mouth?
- What would you change about the organization in your first month on the job if you were placed in charge?
- What examples of learning can you directly relate back to your coursework and what has surprised you in terms of your previous experiences and preparations?

These questions will also allow the student to grow and develop into the type of manager they wish to be. What did you like about your internship and about how the office in which you worked? What did you dislike? Would you like more mentoring? Less? Any number of questions can be asked of yourself and will help you develop your management style.

ORGANIZATION QUESTIONS

Many students do not understand the size and scope of the organizations in this industry. These questions are designed to allow a student to truly understand the structure and operation of the entity for which they are working. Although they can be answered in any order, as the student or internship program may desire, they are laid out in this text as a series of questions answered every two weeks. The answer to these questions will require some research and discussion with those who run the organization. The answers should not be hurried, and each question can be answered more than once.

Journal 1: Organization Management Structure and Operation

- Identify the type of organizational structure utilized
- Locate an organizational chart
- Identify where the internship program fits in the organizational structure
- Where does legal representation appear (in-house or outsourced)?

Journal 2: Human Resources

- Does the organization have a separate HR department?
- Who is the director of HR?
- Develop six questions regarding human resources, such as social media policy and harassment training, and conduct an interview with HR person
- Is the HR department employment an online process?
- Internal or outsourced?

Journal 3: Employment Benefits

- Who coordinates employee benefits for the organization?
- What benefits are available for employees?
- What percentage of the benefits is the employee financially responsible for?

Journal 4: Emergency Action Plan

- Does the organization have an emergency action plan?
- Locate a copy
- What type emergencies are covered? What types are missing?
- What topics are included in the plan?

Journal 5: Organizational Diversity

- What is the diversity makeup of the organization?
- How is diversity managed in this organization?

Journal 6: Annual Performance Evaluations

- Does the organization conduct formal annual evaluations?
- Who conducts them?
- What role do these evaluations play in professional advancement?
- Are the employees offered the opportunity to evaluate their supervisor? The organization?

These questions will also allow the student to understand how organizations require people to "wear" multiple hats. The organizations in this industry are typically very small from an organizational standpoint and require people to help with tasks that in large business organizations may be handled by a whole department such as the human resources department.

BUILDING YOUR NETWORK

Your internship will also offer you the opportunity to continue to grow your network. Much like you did in the research project in Chapter 7, you should spend time with people in your internship organization talking about career topics. These topics are outside the normal questions you would ask to determine why what you are doing is important; instead, these questions revolve around building professional relationships with those you work with. If we go back to the example we used earlier, a networking scenario might go like this:

You are riding to the elementary school for the reading program with the marketing coordinator and director of community relations. You have asked them why the organization has a reading program and what they hope to accomplish with it. Now you can ask questions to help develop a relationship with each of them.

- How each got their start in the industry
- What they look for in a valuable employee
- What makes an intern stand out in a positive way, in a negative way
- What was the best advice they ever received
- What skills they think are critical going forward

The questions asked will be personal to the student and their developing relationships. The student should not stop after just one conversation with each person, as developing the relationship will require multiple conversations. Remember, you want these people to remember you and to remember you in a positive light.

© aelitta/Shutterstock.com

> "The cumulative impact over time of continuing to improve every day results in dramatic change without the drama."
>
> *Danny Morrison • President • Carolina Panthers (2009-2017)*

> "Try to get into as many different projects as you can with a positive attitude and always continue to learn. Identify people who are experts in your chosen field and learn how they became who they are. Try to find a mentor and network. You have a great exciting journey ahead of you, and, with positive attitude, perseverance, and constant learning, you truly have an opportunity to become an expert and a leader in the industry."
>
> *Maria Bordley • HR Director, Employment Marketing and Strategy • Contemporary Services Corporation*

CHAPTER 19

Bringing the Internship to a Close/Evaluation

You have done the work, but how did you do? What did you learn? Where do you go from here? This is the time for a last bit of reflective learning, a final journal entry. Ask yourself the following:

- What did I learn?
- How did my expectations fare against the reality I found?
- How did I do?
- Am I on the right path?

WHAT DID I LEARN?

It is important to list all the skills you have acquired over the term of your internship. This list will come in handy when updating your resume and give you talking points as you continue your networking efforts. From a purely confidence angle, it is good to know what you know. Some things you will be more capable of than others so be sure to be honest, with yourself especially, as you go through the list. Making a claim to have a skill and being unable to deliver can end a career quickly.

What did you learn about yourself in general terms? This is something else it is critical to know. It is one thing to think you can work a ten-game home stand with no break. It is another to know you can. The physical and mental toll on someone in this industry can be very hard to deal with. Going on short sleep, working multiple events over multiple days, and weekends being a thing of the past can wear you out. Knowing you can handle it and not only thrive but enjoy it is a comfort. It will make completing those job applications later much simpler because you are sure you can do it and sure you want to.

EXPECTATIONS VS REALITY

Everyone has an expectation as they head into their internship. Some of the expectations come from their job description and from going through the interview process. Others come from their classroom experiences and information from professors and mentors. Lastly, some expectations come from what they hope or dream their internship will be. This last part is rarely accurate and can cause issues for the student.

This compare and contrast is a great tool for evaluation of the internship. As you work through your expectations be sure to work through why you had them as well. Understanding where the expectations come from can help you control your expectations for future positions and have the expectations grounded in reality.

HOW DID I DO?

This is a simple question, but, for self-evaluation, requires a great deal of honesty with one's self. Your program of study may have a form or other guide to walk you through this process. If it does not, or you are not in a program, one is included at the end of the chapter. This will give you the chance to identify any areas that you should work on going forward, anything that you identified as a weakness. Again, honesty is critical. No one is perfect and everyone can get better.

© nelzajamal/Shutterstock.com

Your program may require it but you will want an evaluation from your supervisor as well. The same form for self-evaluation will work for a supervisor's evaluation if one is not provided. No one likes to hear negative feedback but it is critical to your growth. Ask your supervisor for an honest, critical evaluation of your performance and abilities. This can only help you improve and make yourself more valuable to a future employer. Based on the provided form, ask your supervisor for comments as well. Do not take the feedback personally. It will not be an attack on you and is meant to help you grow as an industry professional. Great feedback, feedback that is actionable, may look like this:

> *The student was always early to work. Willing to do anything that was asked and always looked for extra opportunities. Great attitude! Has the ability to work unsupervised. Always completed assigned tasks in the time required. Would have liked to have seen a little more initiative and taking ownership on tasks she knew were necessary but had not yet been assigned. Needs to work on multitasking as she could not start one project without completing the first. Needs to find her voice. She is very smart and has incredible ideas. Needs to be willing to put herself out there.*

This is a very positive critique with traits that can be worked on and improved. Any intern should be thrilled to receive it. By being willing to take criticism you will make yourself better. If you are not getting better, you are losing ground to others. An evaluation without these types of critical comments is useless.

AM I ON THE RIGHT PATH?

By completing the steps of this critical evaluation, you will learn if this specific field is the one you want. You have done the job. Is it for you? As with every other part of the evaluation process, honesty is critical. Ask yourself the following questions:

- Did I enjoy the work?
- Did I enjoy the atmosphere?
- Am I willing to give my best on this career path?

If you answer yes to these questions, then it is very likely you are on the correct path to start your career. It is important that you like what you are doing, where you are doing it, and that you are still willing to give it everything you have. This is not a career path for those who want to get rich quick. A good salary will come but it is not an overnight happening. Hopefully you had a

© StanislavSukhin/Shutterstock.com

moment in your internship when you realized that, yes without a doubt, this is what I want to do. Maybe it was the look of awe on the face of the young child you read to while wearing the mascot uniform. Maybe it was the energy you felt from the crowd when the house lights came down right before the head-lining band started to play. Maybe it was the look of glee when the little girl in the front row saw her favorite princess in the ice show. Whatever it might have been, if you are in the right field, it will happen.

If you answered no to any of those questions, why? Was it the type of job you had? Was it the people? Hopefully your internship gave you the opportunity to learn about other functional areas that you had not considered. As an example:

> Joe started an internship in an arena with a strong interest in mar-keting but over the course of the internship, while putting in extra time with the operations team, he realized that operations is the job for him. Joe stated, "I love the arena but did not like marketing. I re-ally enjoyed working with the ops folks so that is now my direction."

It all goes back to are you willing to give your best. Answer yes and you have made the right choice.

Be careful evaluating opportunities or organizations based on current employ-ees. Be especially careful using absolutes such as "I would never work for so and so because my boss was not very good." Organizations, even great ones, can have bad people working for them. Maybe you caught someone on a bad day. It could be that someone is just tired or has a situation at home you know nothing about that is causing them stress. Regardless, be careful evaluating an entire organization based on one bad experience. There are not that many jobs in this industry and it would not be smart to eliminate an employer based on one experience. Sometimes a bad employee is an opportunity as well. Here is an example:

> A student is interning with a large crowd management firm. During the course of the internship she works several large events. At these events she often finds her direct supervisor napping in the company office space. She tells her internship coordinator at school about her experience and states she will never go to work for them. Her intern-ship coordinator tells her this is a mistake and she is not looking at it properly.

What does the internship coordinator see that the student does not? Oppor-tunity. Rarely will a large, successful organization not know what is happening within their organization. They will know who is strong, who is weak, and who is dead weight. Seeing a poor supervisor is more opportunity than reason to remove the organization from your list. There are jobs in the industry that many do not aspire to because they do not understand what they are. Because of that, pickings may be slim from candidate pools. The opportunity comes from the organization having a need to replace someone but no qualified candidates to do so.

Last, and perhaps most critical, if you answered no to any of the questions and did not find another aspect of the industry that you wish to pursue, perhaps this industry is not for you. Some will never be able to get beyond their fandom and understand that the job is making sure that others enjoy the show, the game, the band, and not them enjoying the same. This is a hard business because it requires sacrifice. You sacrifice your nights, weekends, holidays, your ability to watch the sport or act you love. You do it, initially, for little pay and less free time. If you have any doubt at all about your desire to make those sacrifices after completing the internship, it is best to go in another direction now.

SUPERVISOR EVALUATION

Please check the number that best represents your opinion of the intern's performance during their appointment. If a two or lower is selected please comment in the space below.

	Poor		Effective		Excellent	
Skills and Abilities						
Possessed necessary technical and/or computer skills	❏ 1	❏ 2	❏ 3	❏ 4	❏ 5	❏ NA
Possessed necessary written communication skills	❏ 1	❏ 2	❏ 3	❏ 4	❏ 5	❏ NA
Possessed necessary oral communication skills	❏ 1	❏ 2	❏ 3	❏ 4	❏ 5	❏ NA
Possessed necessary math skills	❏ 1	❏ 2	❏ 3	❏ 4	❏ 5	❏ NA

	Poor		Satisfactory		Excellent	
Work Habits						
Showed ability to work independently	❏ 1	❏ 2	❏ 3	❏ 4	❏ 5	❏ NA
Thoroughly completed assignments	❏ 1	❏ 2	❏ 3	❏ 4	❏ 5	❏ NA
Showed a sense of responsibility	❏ 1	❏ 2	❏ 3	❏ 4	❏ 5	❏ NA
Was dependable	❏ 1	❏ 2	❏ 3	❏ 4	❏ 5	❏ NA
Showed creativity on assignments	❏ 1	❏ 2	❏ 3	❏ 4	❏ 5	❏ NA
Displayed an ability to work unsupervised	❏ 1	❏ 2	❏ 3	❏ 4	❏ 5	❏ NA

Professionalism						
Exhibited a professional attitude	❏ 1	❏ 2	❏ 3	❏ 4	❏ 5	❏ NA
Could adapt to changing circumstances	❏ 1	❏ 2	❏ 3	❏ 4	❏ 5	❏ NA
Was cooperative	❏ 1	❏ 2	❏ 3	❏ 4	❏ 5	❏ NA
Was punctual	❏ 1	❏ 2	❏ 3	❏ 4	❏ 5	❏ NA
Came to work regularly	❏ 1	❏ 2	❏ 3	❏ 4	❏ 5	❏ NA
Presented an appropriate personal appearance	❏ 1	❏ 2	❏ 3	❏ 4	❏ 5	❏ NA

Other						
Showed a general maturity	❏ 1	❏ 2	❏ 3	❏ 4	❏ 5	❏ NA
Understood the job description	❏ 1	❏ 2	❏ 3	❏ 4	❏ 5	❏ NA

Based on the student's work, what grade would you give them?
(A=Excellent, B=Above Average, C=Satisfactory, D=Below Average, F=Poor)

❏ A ❏ B ❏ C ❏ D ❏ F

If you had the appropriate permanent position available in your organization, would you hire the student?

❏ Yes ❏ No Please comment on why or why not below.

Please comment below on the strengths and weaknesses of the student.

Supervisor's Comment:

SECTION 5

Building on the Experience

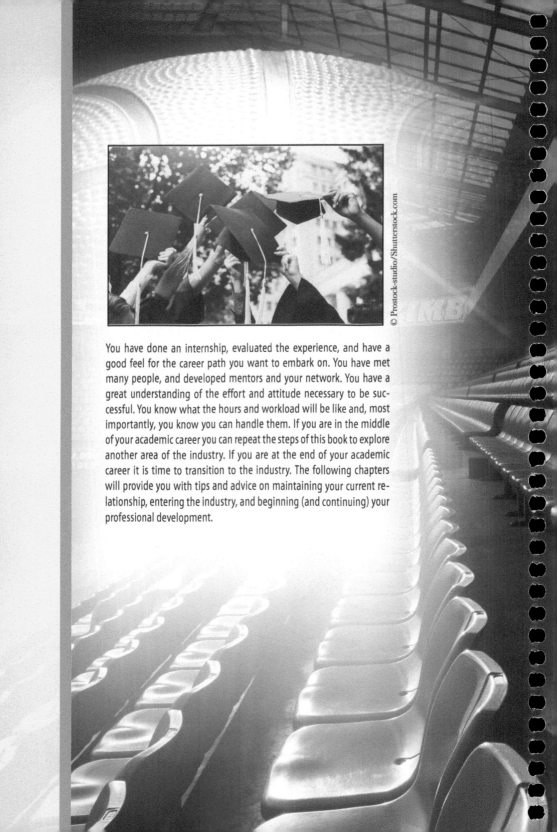

© Prostock-studio/Shutterstock.com

You have done an internship, evaluated the experience, and have a good feel for the career path you want to embark on. You have met many people, and developed mentors and your network. You have a great understanding of the effort and attitude necessary to be successful. You know what the hours and workload will be like and, most importantly, you know you can handle them. If you are in the middle of your academic career you can repeat the steps of this book to explore another area of the industry. If you are at the end of your academic career it is time to transition to the industry. The following chapters will provide you with tips and advice on maintaining your current relationship, entering the industry, and beginning (and continuing) your professional development.

CHAPTER 20

Continuing Relationships

You have created a network through research and working an internship. In the moment these relationships are new and seem strong. You have finished an evaluation from your supervisor and done well. You have made a great impression—but is it a lasting one? You are front and center on your boss's mind but how do you stay there? The worst thing you could do now is to ignore the relationship and think it will be there a year from now. You must do something to maintain, and even build on, the relationship.

One thing you can do to reinforce the relationship is volunteer. You have completed an evaluation with your boss and it is time to head back to school. Are there events coming up that you can work? Maybe it is working a ticket window over the weekend. Doing time in a concession stand. Working on the changeover crew. Even the most menial of tasks can leave a great impression and continue to grow the relationship. If you are too far to drive to the site, are there projects you have been working on that you can continue while at school? Perhaps a marketing plan or making sales calls. Anything to keep you in contact with the organization is a good thing.

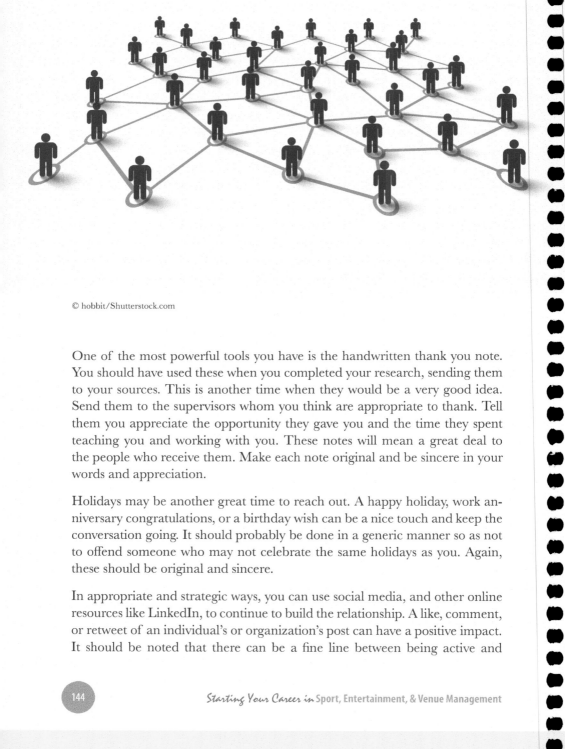

© hobbit/Shutterstock.com

One of the most powerful tools you have is the handwritten thank you note. You should have used these when you completed your research, sending them to your sources. This is another time when they would be a very good idea. Send them to the supervisors whom you think are appropriate to thank. Tell them you appreciate the opportunity they gave you and the time they spent teaching you and working with you. These notes will mean a great deal to the people who receive them. Make each note original and be sincere in your words and appreciation.

Holidays may be another great time to reach out. A happy holiday, work anniversary congratulations, or a birthday wish can be a nice touch and keep the conversation going. It should probably be done in a generic manner so as not to offend someone who may not celebrate the same holidays as you. Again, these should be original and sincere.

In appropriate and strategic ways, you can use social media, and other online resources like LinkedIn, to continue to build the relationship. A like, comment, or retweet of an individual's or organization's post can have a positive impact. It should be noted that there can be a fine line between being active and

© Ruth Black/Shutterstock.com

engaged on social media and stalking. Be smart in your efforts and, if you are unsure where the line is, do not post.

You have been away from your internship site for a little while and you want to reach out to your connections but you do not have a real reason to do so other than wanting to keep the connection up. What reason do you use? Any reason will do. Ask for help on an assignment or to discuss an application to a lesson you learned in class. Perhaps it is a sports franchise that just made a big signing or won a big game or series. Reach out and says congratulations or whatever is appropriate and ask how things are going otherwise. Anything to keep the conversation going and keep you in the front of their mind. To make this even easier, always reply to an old email. You want them to know who you are and, if it has been a little while, this makes it easier for them to recall. Do not make them have to look up who you are.

> "It's a privilege to be able to work in our industry and you should always remember to have fun and enjoy being able to provide memorable experiences to your guests."
> *Josh Harris • Senior Director, Ticketing & Guest Services • Daytona International Speedway*

> "The road to success is never a straight line. Strive to be a leader. Have integrity."
> *Jana N. Brooks • Coordinator, Events & Tenant Services • Maryland Stadium Authority*

CHAPTER 21

Transition to the Industry

You have finished your academic career and begun your search for your entry-level position. In many organizations this position may be yet another internship. It may be a seasonal job, a temporary position, with no guarantee of employment at the end of the term of the contract, meant to run for the organization's full season. It may also be a rotational "training" program. Many who work in the industry worked these types of positions for multiple seasons or years. This chapter will provide some tips and advice on successfully beginning your full-time employment on the career path of your choice.

The new entrant into the industry, if they do not already, must understand the competitive nature of the industry. This book covered this topic earlier, but it needs to be repeated to reinforce the lesson. You will be competing with, potentially, hundreds of other applicants. You could be a top applicant and not receive an interview. This can be very disheartening but you must have persistence if you truly want to work in this industry. Keep applying and interviewing. Keep networking. Keep working the seasonal jobs. Do everything

© mantinov/Shutterstock.com

you can to keep your name out there. You should also understand that you will live better as a college student than you will in your first two or three years working in this industry. Potentially, you have had others helping with your bills. Now they are yours and they come very month. Understand your fiscal reality before you begin to spend the newfound bounty that is your paycheck.

Everyone has heard the phrase, it is not what you know but who you know, and while there is some truth to it, it is full of fallacy as well. It is not, truly, who you know but who knows you. Who has knowledge of your abilities? Who is willing to speak on your behalf? Who is willing to not only make a recommendation but make a phone call on your behalf as well? You may know quite a few people but if they do not truly know you, they will, most likely, be able to offer little in the way of assistance. Lastly, on the what you know component, if you cannot deliver on what you say, word will travel quickly. You will have to know something and be able to deliver it.

There are times, when starting a career, when you will have to make difficult choices. You may take a job outside the industry to pay the bills (or a second job other than an industry job). You may take this position while still volunteering, part-time interning, or working event days only. This can be a very

© Nattakorn_Maneerat/Shutterstock.com

difficult balance and the right choice can only come from the individual in the moment. How much time can I take off from the bill-paying job to chase my dream? Should I ask for time off to attend career expos or recruiting events? Ultimately it will come down to what you are comfortable with and what you are doing to reach your goal of a career in the sport, entertainment, or venue management world.

Once you have started your job, have patience. You have an idea of what the job should be but that is rarely what it is. You know where you want to be but that is definitely not where you start. Show some loyalty and work hard. Do not start looking for the next job the day you start the first. It will come in good time and when you are ready. For some it may happen quickly. For others it may take three to five years to get to a position of real leadership and responsibility. If you continue to work hard and give your best, doors will open. It is at this point in many careers that patience is lost and people leave the industry. You truly need to have a passion for the job to stick it out and be successful.

You are not going to like every boss you have but you can learn from them all. Sometimes it is learning how not to behave, learning how not to treat people, or what not to do. This is another time for the ears open mouth shut mantra.

As with your internship, do not get caught up in office politics or gossip. Also, if your boss is not the best, do not assume those above your boss do not know. Many times the organization may have limited choices and rarely will you know the reasons for all personnel decisions.

A tip for this first job is to do everything you can to make your boss shine regardless of your personal feelings for the person. That is the job you want, right? The best way to it is to move that person on from a successful department. Being a hardworking team player will go a long way toward getting you where you want to be. On the other hand, as you move up the chain, remember to always prepare your people to take your spot. If you make yourself unreplaceable you will never go anywhere. Having people prepared to take your spot allows for growth within the organization. Having that person ready may also lessen the blow of you leaving for another organization. If you can say that so-and-so is ready to take over, and it is true, you reduce the chance of burning a bridge in a small industry.

Be flexible in your selection of destinations you are willing to head to for work. You should be truly open to going anywhere. This will open so many more doors for you. Moving on may be the best way to keep your career moving up.

CHAPTER 22

Never Stop Learning

You have completed the internship and are looking to secure an additional internship opportunity, enter the job market, or seek admission into a graduate program. You will wish to stay relevant and current in the industry of your choice, regardless of your next move.

Your mentors should have offered insight on what journals or books to read; if not, definitely ask them. Hopefully they have also communicated with you concerning professional associations and conferences. Becoming a member of a professional organization, and attending their conferences when feasible, offers a great way for you to stay connected with current issues in the industry and those individuals currently charged with leading the organization through the issues and opportunities.

Often such organizations have reduced rates for students or new members. Membership will usually afford you access to a newsletter outlining current issues and responses. You may have voting privileges and the opportunity to

serve as an officer or student liaison. You may receive as part of your dues, or have the opportunity to purchase at a reduced rate, extra personal liability insurance if it is appropriate for your industry segment.

Conferences, especially in the first years of attendance when you know few people or no one, provide an excellent opportunity for you to get outside your comfort zone. Introduce yourself to persons and look to form connections. Most persons will be happy to meet you, but don't take it personally if a few of the people who are more established in their careers implicitly or explicitly snub you for their friends. Simply move on to the next person!

These conferences are also a great place to continue your knowledge. Many organizations even have industry-specific educational programs that you should take advantage of. Whatever part of this great industry you end up in you should continue to grow. If you stop learning, someone else will pass you by.

Below are examples of organizations that represent many subsets of the sport, entertainment, and venue industry.

International Association of Venue Managers
https://www.iavm.org/

Association of Luxury Suite Designers
https://www.alsd.com/

Venue Management Association
https://vma.org.au/

Association of Outdoor Recreation and Education
https://www.aore.org/

National Recreation and Park Association
https://www.nrpa.org/

National Association of Park Foundations
https://www.the-napf.org/

National Collegiate Athletic Association
http://www.ncaa.org/

National Sporting Goods Association
https://www.nsga.org/

National Association of Intercollegiate Athletics
http://www.naia.org/

Pollstar
https://www.pollstar.com/

Minor League Baseball
https://www.milb.com/

World Esports Association
http://www.wesa.gg/

National Association of Collegiate Esports
https://nacesports.org/

International Association of Convention and Visitor Bureaus
https://www.the-napf.org/

United States Center for Coaching Excellence
http://www.qualitycoachingeducation.org/

Sport Marketing Association
> http://www.sportmarketingassociation.com/

National Federation of High School Sports
> https://www.nfhs.org/

Society of Health and Physical Educators
> https://www.shapeamerica.org/

National Association of Collegiate Directors of Athletics
> https://nacda.com/

The Sports Lawyers Association
> https://www.sportslaw.org/

The International Olympic Committee
> https://www.olympic.org/the-ioc

National Sports Media Association
> https://nationalsportsmedia.org/

College Sports Information Directors of America
> https://cosida.com/

National Alliance for Youth Sports
> https://www.nays.org/

Amateur Athletic Union
> https://aausports.org/

Special Olympics
> https://www.specialolympics.org/

Global Association of International Sports Federations
> https://gaisf.sport/

Billboard Live Music Summit
> https://www.billboardlivemusicsummit.com

Event and Arena Marketing Conference
https://www.eventarenamarketing.com

Canadian Music Week
https://cmw.net/

Aspen Live
http://aspenlive.com

South by Southwest
https://www.sxsw.com/

Pro Sports Assembly
https://www.prosportsassembly.org/

Diversify The Stage
https://www.diversifythestage.org/

Esports Observer
https://esportsobserver.com/

Esports Insider
https://www.esportsinsider.com/

INDEX

Starting Your Career in Sport, Entertainment, & Venue Management

H

Hall of Famer Jack Buck, 48
Hard work, 4
Hockey, 19
Holidays, 144
Hospitality industry, 5
Housekeeping and cleaning services, 38

I

Industry, 3, 147–150
  is transient, 9
  learn by doing and internship, 4
  and research, 56–57
  truly successful in, 4
Industry professional, 6
Industry-specific classes, 15
Institutions, 121–122
Intern-employer relationship, 65–66
International Association of
  Convention and Visitor Bureaus, 153
International Association of Venue
  Managers, 152
International governing bodies, 28–29
The International Olympic
  Committee, 154
Internship
  academic program offering, 4
  and attitude, 116
  benefit of, 4
  classes, 88–89
  completion of, 4
  experiences in, 16
  experiential learning of, 6
  full-time, 44–45
  and law, 61
  multiple experiences, 14
  opportunities of, 120
  positive/negative, 83
  preparations of, 111–114

selection process, 73–74
site, 122
test drive, 49
where to apply, 77–84
when to apply, 85–92

J

Job learning
  journals, 125–127
  networking scenario, 131
Journals
  questions of, 127–131
  tasks/projects, 126

L

Leadership skills, 119–120
Learning skills, 133–134
Life factors
  competing priorities, 74–76
  financial limitations, 69–71
  personal relationships, 72–74
LinkedIn, 100
Live entertainment. *See* Entertainment
  Live shows, 33–34
Living arrangement, 78–79
Long-term volunteer opportunity, 44

M

"Mainstream" sport, 25
Major League Baseball (MLB), 9
"Major league" experience, 80–83
Major League Soccer (MLS), 9
Management/in-house *vs* outsourced
  services, 38
Marketing and media, 39

Student internships
   legal issues of, 801
   and unpaid internships, 65–66
Supervisor evaluation, 139

T

Tasks/projects, 126
Tennis, 23
Theatres, 36
Ticket sales, 38
Toolbox, 7, 86

U

United States Center for Coaching
   Excellence, 153
United States Department of Labor, 5
Unofficial mentors, 122
Unpaid internships and students, 65–66

V

Venue
   arenas and stadiums, 37–38
   conference and convention centers,
     36
   outdoor venues, 36

racetrack, 35–36
   theatres, 36
Venue Management Association, 39,
   153
Volunteer experiences
   full-time internships, 44–45
   long-term volunteer and part-time
     opportunity, 44
   short-term volunteer opportunity,
     41–42

W

WCA. *See* World Cube Association
   (WCA)
WEPF. *See* World Elephant Polo
   Association (WEPF)
Wide-ranging opportunities, 17
World Cube Association (WCA), 29
World Elephant Polo Association
   (WEPF), 29
World Esports Association, 153

Y

YCW. *See* Yogasports Confederation of
   World (YCW)
Yogasports Confederation of World
   (YCW), 29